For all who keep
Christmas;

and for all who read
fairy tales to children.

A Fairy-Tale Christmas

Creating Magical Celebrations
Inspired by an Enchanted Castle

Karen Anderson

Photography
Bryan E. McCay

Decorations at Lyndhurst
R. A. Pesce

Stewart, Tabori & Chang / New York

Produced for Stewart, Tabori & Chang by

High Tor Media, Inc.
Brewster, New York
www.hightormedia.com

Creative Director: Duncan Maxwell Anderson
Graphic Design by Bryan E. McCay

Library of Congress Cataloging-in-Publication Data

Anderson, Karen (Karen Jean)

A fairy-tale Christmas / Karen Anderson; photography [by] Bryan E. McCay.

    p. cm.

  Includes bibliographical references.

  ISBN-13: 978-1-58479-530-8

  ISBN-10: 1-58479-530-1

  1. Christmas. 2. Christmas decorations. I. Title.

GT4985.A59 2006

394.2663--dc22   2006015034

Published in 2006 by Stewart, Tabori & Chang
An imprint of Harry N. Abrams, Inc.

The text of this book was composed in Bernhard Modern BT, LinotypeZapfino, and Gill Sans.

Printed and bound in China

10 9 8 7 6 5 4 3 2 1

harry n. abrams, inc.
a subsidiary of La Martinière Groupe

115 West 18th Street
New York, NY 10011
www.hnabooks.com

Acknowledgments

The idea for this book simply ambushed me one bleak December day when my good friend and co-conspirator Joanne Riccoboni called up and asked innocently, "So . . . are you going to see the Christmas decorations at Lyndhurst?"

I piled the kids into the car and off we went to Tarrytown, New York. I wandered through the house in awe at the imagination and delight packed into every scene. We got to the Little Mermaid's room and my eldest daughter said, "I want my room to look like this!"

I turned to the next museum staffer I saw—Joy Smith—and found myself saying "This should be a book!" She agreed, and told me some names I should call. A fellow visitor overheard and offered a grocery receipt from her purse, just so I could write the names down.

My husband and editor, Duncan, thought this was a hare-brained idea when I came home with it. He also had more confidence than I did that the whole thing would work.

When I interviewed the exhibit's creator, Robert A. (Bob) Pesce, I was delighted to discover an accomplished craftsman whose philosophy of design seems to be based on making people smile. He let me watch him work and answered my questions, as did his crew: David Monzione, Douglas Topper, David McKeown, Chris Martinez, and Adam Lobato. The creation of the exhibit each year is supported by Jan and Warren Adelson.

On a tight schedule, our photographer, designer, and good friend Bryan E. McCay brought the house blooming to life on the page as if he were photographing a beautiful garden (something he also does very well). As we worked with our images, Nemo and Carol Niemann of nemophoto.com gave us invaluable technical help.

Lyndhurst's Director, Jack Braunlein, and the National Trust for Historic Preservation helped with good will and flexibility. Assistant Director Cathryn Anders kept track of everything and regaled us with tales of the house's history. David Ware, Buildings and Grounds Manager, remained helpful even when he and his crew had to work around us. Monica Buller-Cabral inspired me with her observations on the surreal in art, and she moved Lyndhurst's antiques for us a half-inch at a time, several days in a row—nevertheless keeping her sanity.

I have learned much about fairy tales and children's literature from librarian Aili Whalen. She also kept our elf and fairies out of trouble, as did Catherine and Lucy Nathans.

Production coordinator Marie Poe and copy editor Peter Mango graciously kept the rest of us out of trouble. Stylist Yanni Hartman and chef Mark Kaplan performed heroic service on food shoots. My parents and siblings provided family recipes, props, and technical help. Felicity's Tea Room tested recipes. My mother-in-law, Lulu Anderson, playing "Get back in there!" with her giggling grandchildren, showed me that a story begins with interaction.

The expert advice of Marisa Bulzone at Stewart, Tabori & Chang sharpened my focus on fairy-tale food and lore. Countless people, Web sites, books, articles, and creative works have proved crucial to my research. Those that loomed largest are listed on page 158.

My own household of fairy-tale characters has provided inspiration, enthusiasm, and a good audience for my stories, food, and laundry skills. I cannot thank them enough, especially for the Snow Queen's smoothies, Arabian Coffee, and cozy winter fires.

Contents

Once upon a time . . .

I actually inhabit a fairy-tale cottage. It is kind of like the Seven Dwarfs' house, but not as orderly. In our cottage, the Little People are, in descending age order: the Little Mermaid, Rapunzel, Alice in Wonderland, Little Red Riding Hood, and Peter Pan (who is 2).

Besides me, there is one other adult character: Beast (from "Beauty and the Beast")—his transformation into the Prince is *almost* complete. To be fair, I do not usually get myself up in golden dresses and glass slippers either. Beast is sometimes convinced that I am actually the Princess and the Pea, due to my obsession with details no one else cares about; or possibly Sleeping Beauty, owing to my aversion to bouncing out of bed at dawn. The five Little People have concluded that I am Cinderella (i.e., their scullery maid), the Wicked Witch, and the Fairy Godmother, all rolled into one.

Last December, we had an even more horrifying schedule than usual, with long work days right up till Christmas. I dreaded the day it would dawn on the Little People that we had not bought a Christmas tree. Inevitably, on December 21, the "plan-ahead fairies" asked (shrieking) when we would get one.

I suggested *no tree*. I suggested *a "table-top" tree*. I suggested *a fake tree*. I told them to stop believing in fairy tales. I tried to tell them that I wasn't their Fairy Godmother, and I was not going to turn this pumpkin into a gilded coach. I was greeted with betrayed, appalled stares after each of these suggestions. Even Beast gave me a full-blown pout.

And so, at 7:30 P.M. on December 22, we flew the Magic Carpet to our favorite tree source: the parking lot of Stew Leonard's in Connecticut. As we approached the wooden fencing that normally corrals thousands of trees, I looked out on a vast sea of . . . nothing. A huge sign declared: "A Record 15,000 Trees Sold! Thank You!" Anguished wails arose from the back seats of the Magic Carpet.

But the Little People have allies. They believe in St. Nick, and they regularly hit him up for favors. Unfortunately, he often complies. Beast went off to scout, and then returned to the Magic Carpet.

"It's a real 'Charlie Brown' special," he began, "but there is *one* tree left. It's got a big bite out of one side, but maybe you should have a look." I looked. Except for the absolutely huge branch that was missing, it was a great tree—just tall enough to look nice in our low-ceilinged cottage. It stood there bravely in a cute stand. Beast was already cutting deals with the manager, who offered us the tree and stand for less than the price of a tree. *Christmas ornaments were also half price.*

Suddenly I remembered words I often hear from Bob Pesce, who designed the displays you see in this book: "This retails for $ —. Guess how much *I* paid for it!" (The correct answer is always about 90 percent off the retail price.) I started furiously digging around in bins and found some treasures with real class—for example, 60 silvery bead icicles that had never been unpacked. I put together a basket of my finds, and after some back-and-forth with the manager, we got them for close to 70 percent off.

The fairies helped me with the decorating—to keep fights to a minimum, I had them take turns. All the tricks I had learned watching Bob and his assistants made the job easier, much more beautiful, and faster. Instead of using hangers, we wired the ornaments directly onto the branches. There was no time to hot-glue the caps on to make them tamper-proof, so Peter Pan managed to yank two off and smash them before the Wicked Witch turned him into a (sleeping) toad for an hour or so.

The Place Where the Big Branch Wasn't became a spot to put a little scene of ballerinas. The overall result was simple, elegant, imaginative, and fun. It wouldn't have happened if we had used our "dump the ornament box over the tree" approach.

The most wonderful thing about Bob's dramatic decorating style is that a little goes a long way. With a couple of lighting tricks and a few four-dollar bags of fake snow, you can create a world within a room. I explain the basics in "Making Magic" on page 152.

The decorations in this book contain themes, jokes, and allusions. To help you enjoy them more, I included concise adaptations of all the tales, which are the right length for reading to children. They are not all based on the most ancient versions—they are simply the classics everybody likes.

With each chapter I've included Christmas recipes inspired (more or less) by the characters of the tales. You'll find even more recipes, stories, and Christmas lore at www.afairytalechristmas.com. We'd love to hear your comments and suggestions.

Detail, The First Caress *by Guillaume-Adolphe Bouguereau (1866), in Lyndhurst's gallery. In Victorian times, his works were highly sought-after; they enjoy a new surge of popularity today.*

What is the connection between fairy tales and Christmas? It runs deep. The first tales by Hans Christian Andersen and the Grimms were published at Christmas, and were instant best-sellers. *The Nutcracker* and *Peter Pan* premièred at Christmas. The witch's cottage in "Hansel and Gretel" is called a "house of bread"—in Hebrew, that's *Bethlehem.* In "The Snow Queen," Gerda solves Kay's riddle by singing a hymn to the Christ Child.

Christmastime itself seems to put us in the mood for magic. Perhaps when it's too cold to do much outdoors, it's human nature to want to gather by the fire and let our imaginations take flight. To the agnostic, a fairy tale is a way to speak intuitively about magnificence and good will. To the religious believer, it is a poetic way to understand the Creator of the Universe's love for mankind.

It is my fondest hope that you will find something in this book to help you celebrate this beautiful season as your own, and spread your joy to others.

—*Karen Anderson*

Cinderella

A beautiful, gracious young girl lived a peaceful life until her beloved mother died. Her father remarried to a vain and conniving woman who had two daughters of her own.

The girl's stepmother took away everything she owned, including her bedroom, and gave it to her own daughters. From that day on, the poor girl was forced to wear rags and do all the chores. When her work was done, she warmed herself by huddling in the cinders near the chimney. Her stepsisters nicknamed her Cinderella. But she was a hundred times more beautiful in her rags than they were in fine silk and velvet.

Not far away, the prince of the kingdom had to choose a bride, and so all the fashionable people were invited to a grand ball at the palace. Cinderella's stepsisters excitedly began to plan what they would wear. Cinderella was put to work pressing and pleating their dresses, fixing their hair, and giving them advice on how to look their best.

"Cinderella, wouldn't you like to go to the ball?" teased her stepsister.

Cinderella replied, "You know I cannot go."

"Yes, you're right," said the other. "People would laugh to see a cinder-girl at a ball."

Anyone but Cinderella would have fixed their hair badly for spite, but she made them look their best. She watched until they departed for the ball, and then sat down to cry.

"Why are you crying?" asked a voice.

inderella looked up and saw her godmother—who was a fairy—standing in front of her. Through her tears, Cinderella tried to explain her trouble. Her godmother told her: "Be a good girl, and I will make it so that you can go to the ball."

She sent the girl to get a pumpkin from the garden. Cinderella could not imagine how this would help her get to the ball, but she gathered the finest one she could find. Her godmother scooped out the insides and struck the rind with her wand. Instantly it turned into a fine, gilded coach.

Her godmother then asked for six mice from the trap. With a tap of her wand, she turned them into dapple-gray horses. But what would she do for a coachman?

Cinderella said, "I will go and see if there is a rat in the rat trap."

"You are right," replied her godmother. "Go and look." The godmother turned a rat into a fat, jolly coachman, and made six lizards from the garden into footmen with gold-trimmed jackets. As they stood before the grand coach, her godmother asked, "Aren't you pleased?"

"Oh, yes!" answered Cinderella. "But must I go in these nasty rags?"

With a touch of the godmother's wand, the cinder-girl was dressed in a gown of gold and silver, embroidered with jewels. On her feet were the most beautiful glass slippers.

Cinderella got into her coach. Her godmother warned her to leave the ball before midnight, because on the twelfth chime, her coach would turn back into a pumpkin, her horses into mice, and her fine gown into a poor, ragged dress once again.

As Cinderella pulled up, word reached the prince that an unknown princess had arrived. He ran out to help her from her coach and escorted her into the palace. The music stopped and the court grew silent. All that could be heard were whispers of *"How beautiful she is!"*

Above left: Cinderella's chair with her broom. Right: The fairy godmother's chair with her wand. Previous pages, left: The grand mirror and mantle in the Reception Room at Lyndhurst; right: Detail of the ceiling in the same room.

The prince asked her to dance. All the ladies made note of her clothing, resolving to have similar dresses made the next day. Cinderella graciously stopped to talk with her stepsisters, who did not recognize her. The prince could not take his eyes from her all evening. At a quarter to twelve, Cinderella left the ball.

There was a second ball the next night, and her godmother made sure Cinderella arrived in an even more beautiful dress. Cinderella was so delighted with the prince's company that the clock began to strike midnight before she realized how late the hour had grown! She jumped up and fled, nimble as a deer, and the prince could not overtake her. When he reached the gate, the guards told him they had seen only a poor country girl in tattered clothes. But on the steps, the prince did find a little glistening thing—it was one of Cinderella's glass slippers, which had slipped off her foot as she ran.

A few days later, it was announced to the sound of trumpets that the prince was sending a trusted courtier through the countryside with the glass slipper. The prince would marry the girl whose foot fit the slipper.

Cinderella's golden dress, ready for the ball.

When the prince's men arrived at their house, Cinderella's stepsisters tried everything to force their feet into the slipper, but failed.

Cinderella laughed, "Let me see if it will fit me." Her stepsisters thought this was very funny indeed, but the courtier, noticing her beauty, replied that his orders were to try it on everyone. She sat down, and the slipper went on her foot as easily as if it were made of wax. Her stepsisters were shocked still more when she pulled its mate out of her pocket and put it on her other foot.

Cinderella's godmother appeared and changed her rags into a dress even more beautiful than the first two. Her stepsisters suddenly recognized her as the princess from the ball. They fell at her feet to beg her pardon for mistreating her, and she embraced and forgave them.

Cinderella was taken to the prince, who found her still more delightful, and they were married a few days later. They lived happily ever after.

Previous pages: Views of the Reception Room. The top of Cinderella's tree almost reaches the vaulted ceiling.

Below (also shown on page 13): The ceiling above the tree shows a painting of "Dusk" personified, soaring in the twilight with an escort of bats—with the treetop just beyond her fingertips. She seems to be transformed into a Christmas-tree angel.

Above and opposite page, far left: Details from Cinderella's tree. The Cinderella story existed in ancient Greece, India, and China. In each case, a girl loses a single, beautiful slipper, which is found by a king or prince who searches her out and marries her.

Left: In the Grimm brothers' version of "Cinderella," it is a bird perched in a hazel tree over her mother's grave that gives Cinderella her dress and shoes.

There are only two ways to live your life. One is as though nothing is a miracle. The other is as though everything is a miracle.
—Albert Einstein

The Inner Princess

When people talk about a "fairy-tale" ending, they are alluding to Cinderella. Usually, it's to describe a story they think is naive or unrealistic. But that's because they don't understand fairy godmothers.

Superficially, it does look as if Cinderella is handed her future on a platter. But think about it for a minute: All her godmother does is give the girl some new threads and a taxi. It's up to Cinderella to actually get to the ball and act like a princess.

She has to walk very lightly and not trip over decorative urns in her glass slippers—and to avoid wasting time with careless clods who might step on them. Knowing Cinderella, she probably put some duct tape on the soles to keep from landing on her backside while dancing. (Sometimes I wonder what that godmother was thinking . . .)

Mainly, she has to catch the prince's attention and hold it, all the while keeping close watch on the clock, because her finery is temporary. Magic, like all good fortune, can only make obvious what we have already brought to the party.

Cinderella is kind to her stepsisters, returning good for evil. She represents humility: The image of her sitting in the ashes is a parallel with the Greek goddess Vestia, goddess of the hearth. Since there were only twelve thrones on Mount Olympus, Vestia gave up hers so that a thirteenth god, Dionysus, could have it. The quintes-

One of twelve ceiling panels in the Reception Room representing the hours of the day, which were painted in the style of early sixteenth-century Italian frescoes. The original design, probably by Raphael, was in a ceiling fresco in the Vatican. Opposite: Cinderella's tree in the Drawing Room.

sential hostess, she smoothed over an awkward situation, saying that she needed no throne, since her place was at the hearth. This was not because she was a sap or a doormat, but rather the opposite. It was because she did not get her sense of identity or value from changeable things.

Cinderella's confidence, like Vestia's, comes from within. She knows how to be gracious, she knows how to ask for help, she knows how to cry when she hurts—and perhaps most importantly, she knows how to crack a joke.

The prince was no dummy either. When you're the king's son, pretty girls are a dime a dozen. The traits that won him over were the sort brought out by Cinderella's rotten stepsisters, not her dressmaker. He no doubt realized that a sophisticated, resourceful girl who could deal patiently with all kinds of nuts was exactly what he needed in a wife. Consider the difficulties in keeping a kingdom together: There are the relatives out to maim, banish, or kill you so that they can become king. There are the neighboring rulers who wish to enhance their own backyard by moving into yours. There are the peasants ready to revolt if the crops fail. And imagine running a household where visiting noblemen constantly try to steal the silverware.

The prince obviously knew that Cinderella's inner calm and peace would help them get through whatever adversity came their way. It's the inner princess who fits the slipper.

Cinderella's Strategy

Returning from the ball that night, Cinderella had a problem:
Explaining the missing pumpkin and the pulpy mess in the kitchen.
She disposed of the evidence by making these pumpkin tarts.

Destroy-the-Evidence Tarts

This is the recipe found in the palace archives.

Crust:
11/2 cups vegetable shortening
31/2 cups flour
3/4 teaspoon salt
1 glass of water with ice cubes in it

Cut shortening with flour and salt till it makes coarse crumbs. Sprinkle ice water, one tablespoon at a time, lifting dough as you mix. When dough just begins to clump together into a ball (usually after about 6 tablespoons), stop mixing. Divide clump into 18 balls and roll each into a 5-inch circle. Gently press each into a regular or "muffin top" muffin pan. Refrigerate 1 hour.

Filling:
1 cup granulated sugar
1/2 teaspoon salt
11/2 teaspoon cinnamon
1/2 teaspoon each of ginger, cloves, nutmeg, and allspice
1 15-ounce can plain pumpkin

12/3 cup heavy cream
2 eggs, well beaten

Combine sugar, salt, and spices. Add pumpkin, cream, and eggs; beat till smooth. Pour into chilled crusts and bake at 425 degrees for 15 minutes; reduce heat to 350 degrees and bake for another 35 minutes or until custard is set.
Yield: 18 tarts.

Cinderella's Gentle Mimosa

She served these after the ball as a pick-me-up.

Mix together in equal parts: Ruby-Red grapefruit juice, pineapple juice (I use Dole), and seltzer water.
Crush a mint leaf in the drink and add a fresh sprig for garnish.

'Mad Minuet' Sports Drink

After refined exertion, a refined restorative.

Into an 8-ounce glass of seltzer water, squeeze a wedge of lime and stir in 1 teaspoon maple syrup, a pinch of salt, two mint leaves (crushed), and ice to taste.

Above: Pumpkin tarts made from fairy-godmother leftovers. Opposite: Sparkling water with mint, lime, grapefruit, and pineapple, to refresh lords and ladies weary from last night's entertainment.

Rumpelstiltskin

One day, a poor miller bragged to the king that his pretty daughter knew the art of spinning straw into gold.

The king sent for her. She was locked up in a room filled with straw, and told that she must spin it into gold by morning, or she would be put to death.

As night fell, the frightened girl sat alone in the room weeping, for, if truth be told, she could no more spin straw into gold than she could grow wings and fly.

But then a little man appeared in the room, though it had been locked as tight as a drum. He told her that he would spin the straw into gold for her, but what could she give him in return? She gave him the ribbon from around her neck, and the little man set himself to spinning.

The next morning, the king was delighted to find spools and spools of golden thread. But the poor girl was not let go. The king had her locked into a bigger room filled with even more straw and again commanded her to spin it into gold before sunrise. By evening, the girl was about to fall into despair when the mysterious stranger reappeared. In exchange for the ring on her finger, he spun the straw into gold a second time.

The third night, the king put the miller's daughter into an even bigger room filled with straw. This time, he promised to marry her if she succeeded once again.

When the door was locked, the crafty little goblin showed his face. Now he demanded something more valuable: the first child the young woman should bear after she became queen. With hardly a second thought, she agreed, and the room was filled with gold by morning.

A year later, the miller's daughter was settled into her new life, married and a gracious queen. She soon gave birth to a beautiful child.

Like a nightmare come true, the ugly little man appeared at the castle and demanded her baby. Filled with horror, the queen knew she was being called to account for her rash promise. In place of the child, she offered him all the treasure of the kingdom. Shaking his head, he said:

"Something living I like better than all the treasures in the world."

Still, the goblin gave her one more chance: If she could guess his name within three days, she could keep her child.

Rumpelstiltskin's tree. His "spinning wheel" is a nineteenth-century tool for measuring distance.

The queen sent her messenger to scour the countryside for every possible name. The first two evenings, he came back with a host of usual and unusual names, such as Caspar, Melchior, and Baltazar. But none of them belonged to the little man.

On the third day, the messenger went out again, and on his way home discovered a strange place in the forest where animals talk. He spied a ridiculous-looking little man hopping on one foot, chanting a ditty:

Today I brew, tomorrow I bake,
Next morning I shall the queen's child take;
How glad I am that she does not dream
That Rumpelstiltskin is my name!

When the messenger related his story to the queen, she was overjoyed, and rewarded him handsomely.

That evening the goblin appeared to the queen. When she suggested he might be "Conrad" or "Henry," he merely scoffed. She smiled and declared, "then your name is... Rumpelstiltskin!"

The little man screamed, "The Devil told you that!" He stomped his foot so hard that it sank into the earth, dragging the rest of him behind it. Then, with his hands he grabbed his other foot, tearing himself in two.

Rumpelstiltskin's Other Name

Though this folk tale is often interpreted as some kind of psychological fantasy, its odd form more resembles a riddle—one of mankind's oldest forms of literary entertainment. The classic riddle format is to pose a question describing something very familiar—usually an object, force of nature, or living thing—in a way that disguises it. The listener has to guess what it is.

In many myths and folktales, the hero or heroine has to discover the answer to a riddle correctly in order to avert some disaster and gain a reward.

"Rumpelstiltskin" seems to be a double riddle. The tale itself is about a queen who has to guess the answer to a riddle in order to save her child. But the story is also loaded with very specific images that don't seem to make sense. Why does Rumpelstiltskin do such strange things as demand a baby and split himself in two at the end? Are we being asked to guess what his other name is?

Here are some clues we're offered in the tale:

What stands on one leg, has straw and then gold-colored tassels, is ground to powder by a miller, is used in brewing and baking, buries itself in the earth, and finally splits open, thereby ensuring the survival of the next generation?

If you are familiar with Robert Burns's humorous riddle-song "John Barleycorn," about thrashing barley to make whisky, Rumpelstiltskin's real name should be fairly easy—wheat!

The ribbon around the neck of the miller's daughter is perhaps the most interesting allusion. According to an ancient European custom, a "wheat spirit" inhabited each wheat field. During the harvest, the spirit ran from sheaf to sheaf, keeping one jump ahead of the reapers. When the reapers arrived at the last sheaf, a half-dozen young men (called "harvest lads") simultaneously cut it, in a practice called "cutting in common." This was to confuse the spirit and prevent it from taking revenge on the one who did the cutting.

From this last sheaf, a braided wheat ornament was made—a three-dimensional spiral shape called a "neck." The wheat spirit was trapped inside, and one of the young men would run into the house with it, shouting triumphantly. A teenage girl—the prettiest maiden on the farm—would try to tag him on his way to the house. If she succeeded, he was rewarded with a drenching from a bucket of water; if he outran her, he got a kiss.

The neck was hung up in the house and decorated with a red ribbon in honor of Demeter, the goddess of the harvest, whose favorite flower was the red poppy. If the neck was sown the next season, the "wheat spirit" would be released into the field again.

An intriguing coincidence that our ancestors left for us to ponder: Wheat has always been seen as a symbol for the life cycle, encompassing death, rebirth, and fertility. The neck, the oldest type of wheat braid, is made up of several double-helix shapes. Meanwhile, the DNA molecule, whose structure was only disovered in the 1950s, also takes the form of a double helix. Found in every cell of our bodies, DNA is the "blueprint" by which the plan of the human body passes from one generation to the next.

At the end of the tale, Rumpelstiltskin behaves like a grain of wheat—which splits open as it germinates in the earth. The miller's daughter creates gold by giving birth to the next generation.

Anyone who doubts that wheat can turn to gold has never seen a field of grain in the late summer sun.

Rumpelstiltskin's trade secret—a can of spray paint—helped turn this straw into gold. Overleaf: a detail from Rumpelstiltskin's gilded tree.

Rumpelstiltskin's Golden Treats

Chocolate coins are essential for the December holidays. Jewish children get them as Hanukkah *gelt* (gold). Kids in Holland eat them to honor St. Nick. Why make your own? *Better chocolate!*

Golden Treats

The coins that appear mysteriously in children's stockings the night before St. Nicholas's feast (December 6) commemorate the way the saint secretly gave a dowry to three destitute young sisters. According to legend, St. Nick climbed up to the chimney of their father's house one night and tossed in three gold coins (real, not chocolate)—which landed in the girls' stockings, hanging to dry by the fire.

You can easily create your own chocolate treasury and clean up afterward. You can fill your coins with liqueur—or make them with no filling at all. Start by melting a bar of good-quality chocolate according to the directions below. In our opinion, the darker, the better. Our current favorite is Trader Joe's dark Belgian "72 Percent," but we're always experimenting.

   1-pound bar of good dark chocolate
   A small amount of Chambord
     (raspberry) or Cointreau
     (orange) liqueur
   Gold-foil candy wrappers

You will also need:

Newsprint to protect your
work surface (Or, use an aluminum-
   foil–covered cookie sheet)
A coin-shaped candy mold
A candy-making decorator paintbrush
Quart-sized Ziploc freezer bags
A tiny spoon or eyedropper

Break about 4 ounces of chocolate into squares and put it into a quart-sized Ziploc freezer bag. Seal the top of the bag, leaving a little opening for steam to escape. Heat it in the microwave at 40-percent power for about one minute. It is important to heat the chocolate only till just melted; you should still be able to hold the bag comfortably. Knead the bag a little to incorporate any pieces not fully melted and heat it again for 10 seconds if necessary. Snip a shy 1/8 inch from one lower corner of the bag to make a pastry-tip sized opening.
   Holding the bag like a pastry bag, squeeze a lima-bean–sized amount of chocolate into the bottom of each coin mold. Tap the "bean"

Above: All that glitters is not gold, but dark chocolate coins. Previous pages, left: Rumpelstiltskin's tree is visible through a leaded-glass window; right: Ginger ale (left) and ginger-flavored beer.

a few times to settle it in the mold, then swirl it around carefully with a candy decorator brush until the bottom and sides of the mold are fully covered. The chocolate layer should be thick enough that you can't see light through any areas. Let the layer cool at room temperature for a few minutes.

To add liqueur, take an eyedropper or very small spoon and add 3–5 drops of liqueur into the depression in the center of each mold. Using the chocolate bag again, start to cover the coin by squeezing a spiral, working from the sides toward the center. Make sure each loop touches the last fully or you won't cover the liqueur completely, and it will leak out. Gently tap the mold a few times to even out the surface and put the coins in the freezer for a few minutes to harden. To pop out the hardened coins, turn the mold upside down over a plate and twist slightly.

To wrap the coins:

Each coin will be wrapped in a square of foil a little less than twice its diameter (a 1-inch coin will need a wrapper just less than 2 inches square). In most cases, you have to cut the foil down to fit.

Lay the coin, fresh from the freezer, face down in the center of the foil and fold the edges in. Using a light touch, define the face on the front a little and roll the edge to smooth it out.

To make a "coined edge," roll the wrapped coin around the side of a ridged plastic bottle cap.

Yield: 50 to 80 coins.

Ginger Syrup

Rumpelstiltskin reminds me of ginger root: an ugly little thing that makes your eyes water. And yet, the ginger syrup below is one of the best elixirs known to man, and will even help you knock out a chest cold.

Try it poured over applesauce or stirred into tea. Be careful when you enjoy the ginger-and-beer recipe: Like Rumpelstiltskin, it sneaks up on you.

    1 cup fresh ginger root,
        cut into 1/2-inch chunks (peeled,
        if you want a milder drink)
    1 1/4 cups water
    3/4 to 1 cup sugar

Puree the ginger with water in a blender until fine and even, and transfer the mix to a saucepan. Add sugar.

Heat on medium until sugar dissolves—3 to 5 minutes. Once crystals disappear, remove from heat immediately—DO NOT BOIL.

Let it sit for about 5 minutes, pour over a strainer to remove pulp, and refrigerate the strained syrup.

Yield: 2 cups.

Ginger Ale: Pour about 2 tablespoons of syrup over ice in a 10-ounce glass and fill with seltzer water. Add a slice of lemon. (A little mint is nice too, if you have it.)

Ginger-and-Beer: Pour 2 tablespoons of syrup into a 10-ounce glass, add chilled beer and a squeeze of lemon. This works best with a pale brew such as Corona.

Goldilocks and the Three Bears

Once upon a time, a family of three bears lived in a house in the woods. One fair morning they made porridge for breakfast and decided to take a walk while it cooled.

On the edge of the woods lived a little girl who was called Goldilocks because of her pretty golden hair. On that particular morning the sun was shining very warmly through the trees and made lovely pools of light all over the forest floor. Even though she had been warned not to, she started to wander into the woods. Soon Goldilocks had gone quite far.

She was getting a little tired, and not far in front of her there was a funny little house.

She went to the door and knocked. There was no answer, so she went and peeked in the window. Inside she saw a wooden table, and on it were three bowls of porridge with three spoons.

She forgot her manners and pushed the door open. The porridge smelled very good. She went up to the biggest bowl and took just one, tiny little taste. Oooo! It was TOO HOT!

The next bowl was a little smaller. Goldilocks tried a little of that one. Yuck! It was TOO COLD! She threw the spoon on the floor.

She went to the littlest bowl. Oh! It was JUST RIGHT! So she ate it all up.

Now Goldilocks thought she'd sit down by the fire. She tried the biggest chair: It was TOO HARD!

She tried the middle-sized chair. It was TOO SOFT.

Finally, Goldilocks tried the little chair. It was JUST RIGHT.

Above and page 34: The teeny-tiny bear swings on a garland above Goldilocks's head while she naps in the South Bedroom.

$\mathcal{S}$he soon got fidgety and started kicking her feet back and forth. She bounced up and down on the little chair, until POP!—it broke under her, and OOOF!—she flopped onto the floor.

Goldilocks looked around. There was quite a mess. So she left it and climbed up the stairs. At the top she found a funny little bedroom with three beds.

She climbed onto the biggest bed. It was TOO HARD!

She tried the middle-sized bed. She sank down into the feather mattress and was nearly smothered. It was TOO SOFT. But when Goldilocks got to the littlest bed, she found it was JUST RIGHT. She snuggled under the covers and fell asleep.

Meanwhile, the three bears had finished their walk and returned home. They noticed that their door was ajar. They went in cautiously.

The biggest bear saw that his porridge was missing a spoonful and demanded in a great, big-bear voice: "WHO'S BEEN EATING *MY* PORRIDGE?"

The middle-sized bear said in a middle-sized voice, "And who's been eating *my* porridge?"

The teeny-tiny bear saw his empty bowl and said, "Who's been eating *MY* porridge—and EATED IT ALL UP?" Two big tears rolled down his teeny-tiny face.

Then the big bear saw that the cushion was pushed almost off the seat of his chair. He asked, "WHO'S BEEN SITTING IN *MY* CHAIR!"

The middle-sized bear said: "And who's been sitting in *my* chair?"

The teeny-tiny bear said in a very angry, teeny-tiny voice: "Who's been sitting in *MY* chair—and SIT-TED IT ALL UP?"

The bears were quite alarmed and went upstairs. The big bear saw the quilt on his bed all rumpled, and boomed in his big-bear voice, "WHO'S BEEN SLEEPING IN *MY* BED?" His voice sounded like the wind or distant thunder, and it did not wake Goldilocks.

And the middle-sized bear said, "Who's been sleeping in *my* bed?" It sounded like someone talking in a dream, and it did not wake Goldilocks.

When the teeny-tiny bear saw the shiny, golden hair of Goldilocks on the pillow, he said in a teeny-tiny voice, "Who has been sleeping in *MY* bed—and lies there still?"

The teeny-tiny bear's voice was so sharp and shrill, it sounded like the buzzing of a bee right in Goldilocks's ear. She sat up and saw THREE BEARS standing over her.

Goldilocks tumbled off the other side of the bed, ran to the window, and jumped out. When she reached the ground, she did not stop running until she was back at her mother's house.

Tales and Toddlers and Bears—Oh My!

Some fairy tales are beautifully constructed works of art written by a single author such as Hans Christian Andersen or Lewis Carroll. Others are folk tales handed down centuries ago by grandmothers to their grandchildren. Telling tales is what people did to keep kids out of mischief before television.

Face-to-face storytelling does a number of important things: It gives family members something to do together. It teaches the children about the lessons of the world in a way that is so entertaining that they don't realize they are learning useful truths. And it gives even the dullest adult an audience on which to practice his comic delivery and acting skills.

"Goldilocks and the Three Bears" is obviously intended to be read to others. You just can't tell it without making your voice BIG, middle sized, or teeny-tiny at the appropriate points. One of the earliest published editions had the dialogue printed in different-sized type for each of the three bears.

If this story is read in the proper spirit, after the first telling, the narrator will be asked to "read it again" 247 times. If the listener is teeny-tiny, he may simply squeal, "Uh-*DEN!*"

Telling tales, the original "interactive theater," calls for keen attention to the tastes and enthusiasms of the audience. If there is a bunch of boys in the audience and the story is only about being kind and sensitive, or if it features too many princesses and not enough sword-fighting, the boys will start flicking paper-clips at each other or playing with a spider that just crawled across the floor.

But if you then mention a gory accident or two, they will elbow each other to be quiet and give you their rapt attention.

If you have an audience of girls and you tell them about too many battles, they will start to look out the window or need to go potty suddenly. The right fairy-tale for a mixed audience has a good balance of both kinds of drama.

Why do children love "Goldilocks and the Three Bears"? It first became popular around the middle of the nineteenth century, when people who lived near wooded areas were a little more familiar with bears than they wanted to be. To this day, many bears have poor manners, and will take the tops off garbage cans or remove the doors from cars or refrigerators just for a snack.

In this tale, the situation is reversed: It is a family of bears whose nice little house is reduced to chaos. In the earliest versions of the story, the invader was a fox or an old woman. But someone figured out a way to make the plot even funnier. Imagine a group of huge, wild animals confronted with the only creature more destructive than they are: a misbehaving toddler.

Above and overleaf inset: The bears' tree in the South Bedroom. Overleaf: Goldilocks and the Three Bears celebrate Christmas in the mansion's Northwest Bedroom. Their tree is decorated in a woodsy riot of pine cones, acorns, and forest creatures. A few lilac-colored birds added to the gold, rust, and olive green ornaments give it an extra flourish.

Breakfast in the Woods

In the early morning, the delicious aroma of wild blueberries:
This oatmeal is much more than cereal, and hearty enough for a bear.

The Bears' Oatmeal Porridge

If you really want to know what bears eat for breakfast, I can tell you on good authority that they like hazelnuts and chestnuts. But they just LOVE wild blueberries (also known as huckleberries). It is therefore always a good idea to use caution when picking them for your own breakfast!

2 cups rolled oats (the quick-
   cooking or 5-minute variety)
4 cups water
1 large apple, peeled and cut into
   thin slices (approximately 1 cup)
Salt to taste

Toppings:
Hazelnuts
Roasted Chestnuts
Dried wild blueberries
Any combination of butter, cream, maple
   syrup, brown sugar, cinnamon, etc.

In a saucepan, combine oats and water. Shake the pan a little and remove any bits of husk that float to the top. Cook at medium heat for 3–5 minutes. Add apples and continue cooking until thickened—about 5 minutes more. Time is approximate—cook until apples are moderately soft. Remove from heat and let cool slightly before serving.
   Yield: about 6 servings.

Teeny-Tiny Bear's Tea

One day a little bear in our house was feeling under the weather, so Mamma Bear served her this tea. The little bear philosophically observed, "Even though this is the worst day of my life, this is the best tea I ever tasted."

For each cup (adjust to taste):
1 cup water heated to just boiling
1 bag Celestial Seasonings Sleepy-
   time tea (chamomile/spearmint)
1 heaping teaspoon honey
2 teaspoons cream
Ground cinnamon (Frontier organic
   is especially nice; it has a little
   oil in it so it floats on top.)

Steep tea bag in water for five minutes. Stir in honey and cream; sprinkle top with cinnamon and serve immediately.
   Yield: 1 cup.

Above and opposite: The teeny-tiny bear's SECOND bowl of porridge. To make up for the one Goldilocks ate, it is served in his very own silver porringer and has his favorite treat on top: roasted chestnuts, hazelnuts, and dried wild blueberries.

41

Hansel and Gretel

A poor woodcutter lived on the edge of a great forest with his two young children and their stepmother.

A famine came upon the land, and the woodcutter did not even have enough food to give his family bread for their meal. He fretted day and night until at last his wife said: "Let us go very deep into the forest and bring the children with us. When we have gone quite far, we will build a fire for them and leave them there. They will not find their way home and we shall be rid of them."

The woodcutter objected: "They will surely be torn to pieces by wild animals."

She replied, "That would be better than all four of us dying of hunger." And she gave her husband no peace until he reluctantly agreed.

Now, all of this was overheard by the children, who were so hungry they could not sleep. The girl, whose name was Gretel, began to weep.

Hansel, her brother, said, "Shhh! Do not be afraid. I will find a way to help us." After the moon rose, he sneaked outside, where the small white pebbles shone like new silver pennies, and stuffed his pockets with them. He returned to his bed and said to Gretel, "Be comforted, dear little sister, and sleep in peace. God will not forsake us."

The next morning before the sun rose, the woodcutter's wife woke the children and gave them each a piece of bread, scolding them: "Get up, you sluggards! We are going into the forest to fetch wood."

Along the way, Hansel walked behind the others and kept stopping to drop pebbles one by one behind him. When they were deep in the forest, the woodcutter built a fire and told the children to rest while he and his wife gathered fuel. While the children slept, the woodcutter tied a piece of wood to a tree so that the sound of it knocking in the wind would make them think he was nearby, chopping wood.

When Hansel and Gretel awoke, it was dark and they were alone. But the moon rose and the children followed the trail of white stones, arriving home at daybreak. Their father was overjoyed to see them, but his wife scolded them for sleeping so long in the forest.

There soon came another famine, and the woodcutter's wife again persuaded him to lose the children deep in the woods—this time for good. The night before their trek was to start, she locked the house so that Hansel could not gather white stones.

As the family trudged into the forest, instead of stones, Hansel stopped to drop little crumbs of bread in the path. But alas, when night fell and Hansel and Gretel tried to find their way back, they found no crumbs, for the birds had eaten them all. Now truly lost, they passed two nights in hunger and fear.

At midday of the third day, a beautiful, snow-white bird came to sit on a nearby branch, singing sweetly. The bird led the children to a little house in the forest made of bread and covered with cakes, with windows of clear sugar. Hansel told Gretel to start eating the windows, while he began pulling pieces from the roof. They had no sooner begun than they heard a quiet voice calling from the parlor:

"Nibble, nibble, little mouse,

Who's that nibbling on my house?"

Without stopping, the children answered:

"The wind, the wind,

The heaven-born wind."

Suddenly, the door swung open, and a woman as old as the hills appeared. She had red eyes and walked with two crutches. Hansel and Gretel were frightened, but she told them not to fear. She took the children by the hand and led them inside to a delightful meal of milk and pancakes with sugar, apples, and nuts. Afterward, she told them to rest on two pretty little beds covered in white linen. The children fell asleep and thought they were in heaven.

But the old woman was a wicked witch. When morning came, she locked Hansel in a stable and said to Gretel, "Fetch some water and cook something good for your brother. I wish to make him fat, so that I may eat him."

Lyndhurst's old cookstove—a bad place for witches. Opposite: Over the stove, a wreath with faux fruit and candy. Page 43: A garland over the kitchen cabinets.

Hansel was richly fed. Each morning, the witch ordered him to poke his finger through the stable door, so she could feel how fat he'd grown. Each time, he held out a thin sliver of bone from his plate instead, and she was fooled into feeding him for another day.

After four weeks, the witch grew impatient and commanded poor Gretel to boil a pot of water to cook her brother. The witch added that she had lit a fire in the oven to bake bread, and Gretel must creep inside to see if it were hot enough.

The little girl saw what the witch had in mind and asked, "But how can I fit?"

The witch replied, "Silly goose, the door is big enough. See? I can get in myself!" So eager was she to entice Gretel into the oven that she thrust her own head in to show her how. At that, the little girl gave a mighty push, and bolted the oven door shut with the witch inside.

Gretel ran like lightning to let Hansel out of the stable. The two children danced and hugged each other joyfully. In the witch's house, they found chests of pearls and jewels in every corner. Hansel stuffed his pockets and Gretel filled her apron, and they set off in haste to find their way home. Their way was blocked by a wide stretch of water, but Gretel saw a white duck, and called out to it:

Little duck, little duck, dost thou see? Hansel and Gretel are waiting for thee.

There's never a plank or bridge in sight; Take us across on thy back so white.

The good little duck swam to them and took them one at a time to the other side.

There, the woods at last began to look familiar. They saw their father's house and began to run, and did not stop until they had rushed into the parlor, into his arms. He was beside himself with joy. He had not known one happy hour since leaving them in the forest. His wife, however, was dead.

Gretel emptied her apron and Hansel tossed out handfuls from his pockets until pearls and precious stones tumbled all over the floor. From that day on, they were anxious no more, and lived together in perfect happiness.

A Candy Cottage

Candy Christmas decorations, even when not edible, are delightful. Walk into a room filled with colorful candy garlands, sugared fruits, and iced cookies, and you will smile.

Above: Garlands and ornaments of faux fruit are unwrapped and organized into separate piles for hanging.

Left: Faux-gingerbread cookie ornaments. These will be divided into equal groups so they can be spaced evenly on the garlands.

Below: Blown-glass slices of cake and cone-shaped trees aren't good to eat, but they last longer than their real counterparts, and they don't leave crumbs.

When at night
I go to sleep,

Fourteen angels
watch do keep.

—Adelheid Wette
From the Engelbert Humperdinck
opera, Hansel and Gretel, *1893*

Sugar and Spice

She may have needed a different attitude, but you have to admit,
the witch could cook. I think if she'd opened a bakery and sold these,
she might have become the most popular girl in town.

Gingerbread Cookies

*Not every present sits under the tree. At least
one December day, you MUST bake gingerbread—
because the aroma alone spreads such good cheer!*

1/4 cup unsalted butter, softened
1 cup brown sugar
1/3 cup maple syrup
31/2 cups flour
1 teaspoon salt
2 teaspoons ground ginger
2 teaspoons ground cinnamon
1 teaspoon baking soda
1/2 teaspoon vanilla extract
1/4 cup chopped crystallized ginger

In a large bowl, cream butter and
brown sugar. Add the maple syrup,
continuing to stir until creamy.

Add flour, salt, ginger, and cinnamon.

Add baking soda, vanilla, and 1/2 cup hot
water. Mix until smooth, but not sticky. If necessary, add more flour. Stir in chopped ginger.

On parchment paper, roll out dough
to about 1/8 inch thick.

Cut with shaped cutters into your
choice of creatures (men, birds, hearts,
Christmas trees, stars, harps . . .) and transfer to a parchment-lined baking sheet.

Bake at 350 degrees for 10–12 minutes.
Yield: 2–3 dozen cookies.

*A delicious and quick icing to pipe on your gingerbread cookies: Mix 1 cup confectioners
sugar with 1/2 tablespoon soft butter, 2 tablespoons maple syrup, and 1 teaspoon cream.*

Little Red Riding Hood

There once was a little girl so charming that she was loved by everyone she met. Her grandmother made her a cloak with a red velvet hood; it was so becoming it earned her the nickname "Little Red Riding Hood." If the little girl had one fault, it was that she didn't always do exactly as she was told—and that is how she ran into trouble with the Wolf one day.

Red's Grandma was feeling ill, so her mother gave her a basket with some cakes and a little wine to bring to her house, which was a little farther than the village, about a half-mile away. Red's mother warned her quite firmly to go right away, and not to wander off the path into the woods.

The story would end right here if Little Red Riding Hood had continued along the path as she was told. But Red hadn't gotten very far when she met a Wolf and stopped to talk with him. She told him exactly where she was going and why. The Wolf was interested in lunch, and decided that, although Red would be very tasty, she might not be enough by herself. So he plotted to eat both Red and her grandmother. He pointed to some pretty flowers in the woods and suggested that Red leave the path to gather some for Grandma.

Off went Red in search of some pretty little flowers. Now, the Wolf knew that the more flowers you collect, the more you want, and the best ones are always a little farther ahead. He watched until Red was a good way from the path, and then trotted ahead to Grandma's.

He knocked on her door and imitated Little Red's cute little voice.

"Come in," Grandma said, whereupon the Wolf rushed in and ate her up.

Then he put on Grandma's nightcap and nightgown, climbed into her bed, pulled the covers way up to his chin, and waited for Red.

Meanwhile, Red had gathered as many flowers as she could carry, so she made her way to her grandmother's and knocked. Using his best "Grandma" voice, the Wolf told Red to come right in.

Little Red thought Grandma's voice sounded a little husky, but supposed it must just be her cold. So she went in. She sat down on the bed and noticed a few odd things:

A carved detail on the hall tree in Lyndhurst's foyer. Previous page: A vignette from Red's tree.

"Grandma?"

"YE—*Yes, dear?*"

"Grandma! What great big ears you have!"

"The better to HEAR you with, my dear."

"And what big eyes you've got!"

"The better to SEE you with, my dear."

"And Grandma, what big hands you have!"

"The better to HOLD you with, my dear."

"—But Grandmother!" cried Red, who was beginning to be a little frightened, "what great big TEETH you have!"

"THE BETTER TO EAT YOU UP!" cried the Wolf, jumping out of the bed. He gulped up poor Red in one mouthful.

Now the Wolf was tired. He settled in for a nap, and soon began to snore very loudly.

A hunter happened to pass by the cottage, and heard the awful racket. "Oh dear," he thought to himself, "how the old woman snores! I must go in and see what is the matter."

So he stepped into the cottage and saw the Wolf lying on the bed. "Oh, you old sinner!" he cried. "Have I found you at last? I have been looking for you a long time, Mr. Wolf!"

He was about to raise his gun to his shoulder when he noticed that Grandma was not in her house as she should be. He put down his gun and took up a pair of scissors instead. When he cut the Wolf's stomach open, how surprised he was to see Little Red's smiling face peer out!

"Oh, I have been so frightened, it was so dreadfully dark in the wolf's stomach!" cried Red.

He kept cutting and found her grandmother, who was also unhurt.

Little Red, Grandma, and the hunter sat down very contentedly to a meal of the wine and cakes that Red's mother had made. Then the hunter took Red safely home.

Life in the Trees

This tree is decorated in a classic woodland theme, with the emphasis on a rich red color and things that go well with it, like white birch bark-covered balls (page 53 and at right). Pheasant feathers are generously wired onto the branches, a reminder of the hunter who rescues Red and her grandmother. Below are Red's cloak and picnic basket, being guarded by Mr. Wolf.

This small tabletop tree is rich in impact; you can practically hear the birds as they chatter and flit among the branches—ready to erupt into a flurry of wings if you move too suddenly! At 4 feet tall, it is perfectly scaled to make use of a hallway corner where a full-sized tree would be in the way.

The window beyond the tree is graced with a small garland that keeps the focus upward—like the view Red would see in the branches above her.

Art and Nature: Near the base of Little Red Riding Hood's tree, the branches have been separated and bent to make a hollow space or niche—creating a little stage where the ornaments become characters in their own little play. In this case, a family of partridges has taken up residence in a nest placed there.

This technique of creating a diorama in the branches of a tree is also useful for hanging a particularly large or showy ornament, or one that looks best suspended freely without catching on anything below it. While it is

easiest to bend the branches of an artificial tree like this one, sometimes a real tree has a naturally occurring bare spot that can be put to good use as a stage for an ornament scene instead of being hidden in the back.

Decorative materials and ornaments you use can be either bland and predictable or wonderfully engaging, depending on how you place them. Using bird, animal, or human figures, you can give a feeling of animation by "posing" the figures—as children do when playing with their toys and dolls, making them do things and talk to each other. Freeze that kind of action right on the tree, and add accessories you'd expect to see accompanying it.

The liveliness of Little Red's tree is heightened by artistic touches that mimic the way real birds act. The faux birds are wired closely onto the branches so they look as if they are really perched there—if only for a moment. Some of their heads are oriented out toward us. Others point toward other objects on the tree—sizing up a seedpod or bit of nesting material. One bird has a dried twig hot-glued to his beak; another has her head cocked to inspect her eggs.

Another way to improve ornaments is by modifying them. Give them things to hold, add a little glitter, remove an ugly bow, or change the surface with paint. You may be surprised at the power in your hands. Delighted viewers see a tabletop that seems to come twittering to life.

Pheasant feathers crown the top of Little Red's tree in honor of the hunter. Overleaf, left: A little bird rests for a moment; right: The deep red of the tree's cranberries and pomegranates is set off by the complementary colors of acorns, pine cones, and chartreuse balls.

Little Red Riding Hood's Picnic Lunch

Traditional poppy-seed cakes and a country wine concoction
will help Grandma and all her grown-up friends get ready for spring.

Lemon Poppy-Seed Cakes

Here are the cakes from Red's basket.

1 1/2 cups flour
1 1/2 cups rolled oats
1/2 teaspoon salt
1 tablespoon baking powder
1/2 cup (1 stick) unsalted butter, softened
1/4 cup sugar
1 egg
Grated zest of one lemon
Juice of one lemon (1/4 cup)
1 tablespoon poppy seeds
Heat oven to 400 degrees

In a large bowl, mix flour, oats, salt, and
baking powder. In another bowl, whisk together
butter, sugar, egg, and lemon zest. To com-
bined dry ingredients, add butter mixture and
lemon juice; add poppy seeds and mix lightly.

Turn out onto a lightly-floured surface and
knead a few times, adding flour if too sticky. Pat
or roll to about 5/8 of an inch thick; cut rounds
with a 2 1/4-inch biscuit cutter or thin-rimmed
glass. Place on an un-greased cookie sheet
and bake at 400 degrees for 10–12 minutes.

Yield: 12–16 cakes.

May Wine

*This delightful concoction is made with an herb
common to northern forests, sweet woodruff or
waldmeister (master of the woods), available at
nurseries in the U.S. In Germany, it is used to help
relieve headaches, and I am quite sure that this is
the wine that Red's mother sent over to Grandma's.
It would soon have had the lady feeling quite plucky.*

1/4 cup tender, new, sweet woodruff leaves,
    or 1 ounce dried leaves (about 2/3 cup)
2 tablespoons sugar
1 bottle of Rhine wine (750 ml)
1/2 cup brandy
1 bottle sparkling wine
1 cup strawberries
Slices of fresh orange (optional)

In a ceramic or glass bowl, mix the
leaves, sugar, brandy, and wine. Cover
tightly and refrigerate overnight. Strain the
mixture into a punch bowl, add the champagne, and garnish with strawberries and
orange. Note: milder versions are made by
omitting the brandy or by substituting car-
bonated water for the sparkling wine.

Yield: 10–12 glasses.

Above: Poppy-seed cakes made from rolled oats. Opposite: They go beautifully with strawberries and May wine.

Snow~White

Once upon a time in midwinter, when the snowflakes fell like feathers from heaven, a beautiful queen sat embroidering at her window, which had a frame of black ebony. She pricked her finger with her needle, and three drops of blood fell into the snow.

She thought, "If only I had a child as white as snow, as red as blood, and as black as ebony wood." Soon afterward she had a little daughter as lovely as her wish; they called her Little Snow-White.

As soon as the child was born, the good queen died.

A year later the king took himself another wife, beautiful but vain. Often she would stand before her magic mirror and ask:

Mirror, mirror, on the wall,

Who in this land is fairest of all?

To this the mirror answered:

You, my queen, are fairest of all.

Then she was satisfied, for she knew that the mirror spoke the truth.

Snow-White grew up and became ever more beautiful. When she was seven years old she was as beautiful as the light of day—even more beautiful than the queen.

One day when the queen asked her mirror who was fairest, it answered:

You, my queen, are fair, it is true.

But Snow-White is a thousand times more fair than you.

When the queen heard this, she grew pale with envy, and from that hour, she hated Snow-White. The vain woman knew no peace, day or night.

Finally she summoned a huntsman and commanded him to take Snow-White into the woods and kill her, bringing back her lungs and liver as proof. But once in the woods, he took pity on the poor girl and let her go. He killed a young boar instead, cut out its lungs and liver, and took them back to the queen.

All alone in the great forest, Snow-White ran all day over thorns and sharp stones until she came to a little house. She went inside and found everything neat and orderly. There was a little table with seven little plates and spoons, seven little knives, forks, and mugs; against the wall there were seven little beds, all freshly made.

Snow-White was hungry and thirsty, so she ate a few vegetables and a little bread from each little plate, and from each little glass she drank a drop of wine. She was tired, so she said her prayers and fell asleep in one of the beds.

When night came, the seven dwarfs who lived in the cottage returned home from their work in the mines. They lit their seven little candles and saw that someone had been in their house, eating the food at their table.

Above and page 57: It's Christmas Eve, and Snow-White has hung the dwarfs' boots on the mantel, awaiting a visit from St. Nick. For the pattern, see "Sources," page 158.

Then one of the dwarfs found Snow-White lying in his bed, fast asleep. The others came running. "Good heaven!" they cried. "She is so beautiful!" They did not wake her up, but let her rest.

When Snow-White woke up and told them how she had come there, the dwarfs said, "If you will keep house for us, and cook, make beds, wash, sew, and knit, and keep everything clean and orderly, then you can stay with us, and you shall have everything that you want."

"Yes," said Snow-White, "with all my heart."

Every morning they went into the mountains digging for ore and gold, and in the evening when they came back home, she had their meal ready. During the day she was alone.

With Snow-White gone, one day the wicked queen consulted her mirror to learn who was fairest in the land. She was shocked when it replied:

You, my queen, are fair; it is true.

But Little Snow-White beyond the seven mountains

Is a thousand times more fair than you.

Because only the seven dwarfs lived in the seven mountains, the furious queen knew that they must have rescued her. She vowed, "Snow-White will die, if it costs me my life!"

She made a poisoned apple, disguised herself as a peasant woman, made her way to the dwarfs' cottage, and knocked on the door.

"I am selling these apples, and I will give you one to taste."

"I can't let you in. The dwarfs have told me to speak to no one."

"If you are afraid, then I will cut the apple in two and eat some of it. Here, you eat the beautiful red half!" When Snow-White saw the peasant woman eating from the apple, her desire for it grew, so she finally took it and tasted it. But the red half was poisoned, and immediately she fell down dead.

That evening the dwarfs returned home from the mines and saw Snow-White lying on the floor. Nothing they could do would revive her; she was dead. They laid her on a bier, and all seven sat next to her and cried and cried for three days. They said, "We cannot bury her in the black earth," and they made her a glass coffin, so she could be seen from all sides. They laid her inside, and in golden letters wrote her name, and that she was a king's daughter. They put the coffin outside on a mountain, and one of them always stayed with it and watched over her.

Creatures came and wept for Snow-White—first an owl, then a raven, and finally a dove. Snow-White lay in the coffin a long, long time.

One day, a young prince on a hunt came to the dwarfs seeking shelter for the night. He saw beautiful Snow-White on the mountain in her coffin, and he read what was written on it. He asked to buy the coffin, but they refused. Then he begged them to give her to him, for he could not live without seeing her; he promised to honor her as his most cherished thing on earth. Taking pity on him, they gave him the coffin.

The prince had his servants carry away the coffin on their shoulders. One of them stumbled, dislodging a piece of poisoned apple from Snow-White's throat. She opened her eyes, lifted the lid from her coffin, and sat up—alive!

"Good heavens, where am I?" she cried out.

The prince said joyfully, "You are with me." He told her what had happened, and then said, "I love you more than anything else in the world. Come with me to my father's castle. You shall become my wife." Snow-White loved him, and gladly went with him.

The wicked queen's jealousy drove her to go to the wedding. Two iron shoes were put into the fire until they glowed, and she had to put them on and dance in them. She could not stop until she had danced herself to death.

Lovely, Dark, and Deep

One of the reasons a great fairy tale lives for centuries is that it keeps calling us back. Its images are so compelling, you can almost touch them. And the deeper you look, the more you find. This is especially true of the Grimm tales.

Jakob and Wilhelm Grimm relied on a vast range of inspirations for the tales they began publishing in 1812. Their sources included sketchy German folk tales a few paragraphs long, Norse myths, entire medieval epics like *Parzival*, and the Bible. The brothers were medieval scholars fluent in many languages, ancient and modern.

The Grimms even drew on tales published in the eighteenth century by such forgotten writers as Giambattista Basile and Johann Karl August Musäus, which are characterized by crude jokes, irony, and cynicism. You could almost call them "anti-tales," resembling the many wise-acre retellings of classic tales found all over the Internet today. They typically portray heroes and heroines as dupes or predators. They seem to be fairy tales for the enlightened, with all the magic and virtue safely explained away to avoid offending delicate rationalist sensibilities. Basile's Cinderella murders her first stepmother. Musäus's Snow-White ("Blanca") is given a narcotic instead of a poison: The prince doesn't bring her back to life, so much as bring her out of a drug-induced stupor.

The Grimms' view of fairy tales was different. Instead of seeing them as mildly amusing diversions, they believed they could speak to the deepest yearnings of the human heart.

"Snow-White" in the Grimms' hands becomes a poetic retelling of the fall and redemption of man from Genesis to the New Testament—a close parallel of

Every single ornament and bead chain on Snow White's tree is red. The sparkly ones are tempting, faux sugared strawberries and other fruit. The rest are, of course, apples.

Milton's *Paradise Lost*. The evil queen in "Snow-White" plays the same role as Milton's Lucifer, the most beautiful of the angels in heaven. Like the queen looking into her mirror, he seethes with envy when he learns of the creation of mortal human beings. The deadly apple plays its familiar part in both stories.

Look at how Snow-White is described: "white as snow, red as blood, and as black as ebony." Since medieval times or earlier, white has represented purity and the soul, and red has stood for the human heart: for love, emotion, and sacrifice. Black has been associated with death and mortality. Snow-White represents human nature itself: supernatural, loving, and at the same time, mortal. The tale makes much of the fact that she is beautiful even after she has fallen and died. Instead of hiding her away, the dwarfs place her coffin on top of a mountain, unashamed of her helplessness in death.

The dwarfs mourn, guard, and commend her body to providence. After a long time, the King's son finds her, declares he cannot live without her, and brings her home to his father's house to be his bride.

It is clear that that Wilhelm Grimm thought deeply about death and resurrection. Something of a mystic, he also suffered from a terrifyingly painful heart ailment that sometimes kept him awake all night, physically and emotionally exhausted. When he heard the call of his neighbor's pet quail to announce the sunrise, he knew that he, too, had survived to greet another day.

The Greek New Testament that Wilhelm frequently read in the morning had 71 passages underlined in a fine quill pen. One of the highlighted passages contains the words Christ spoke to Martha moments before he raised her brother Lazarus from the dead: *"I am the resurrection and the life."*

*Right: Snow-White's
tree in the East Bedroom.
Artificial snow billows out
from under the tree—in-
stead of a standard tree
skirt—and it's topped with
a felt hat donated by one
of the Seven Dwarfs. To
the left of the tree is an
antique wagon-sled, filled
with a load of burlap bags.
I imagine they contain gold,
silver, rubies, and diamonds
the dwarfs have mined
from deep under the earth.*

*Little clumps of
artificial snow are also laid
on the branches (they don't
need to be secured in any
way), imitating the look
of a real tree just after a
snowfall.*

*Previous page: Snow-
White has also been a
guest in the Northeast Bedroom. Here the "snowdrifts"
blow into the room from
behind a dresser in the corner. The snow is bordered
with faux pine garlands
and pine cones, just visible
at bottom right.*

*For thou wilt lie
upon the wings
of night,*

*Whiter than
new snow upon
a raven's back.*

—*William Shakespeare,*
Romeo and Juliet

62

Apples Overturned

At the wedding, the prince's chefs served a special dessert
of apple turnovers and hot cider. Snow-White, the prince, and
the dwarfs all found it amusing, but the evil queen did not.

Snow-White's Turnovers

Pastry

2 cups flour
1 teaspoon salt
2/3 cup shortening
Ice water
White of 1 egg
1 teaspoon sugar

Filling

4 large apples, pared, cored, and cubed
1/2 cup brown sugar
1/2 teaspoon cinnamon
1/2 teaspoon nutmeg
1 wedge of lemon

Mix flour with salt; cut in shortening. When mix is crumbly, add ice-cold water, 1 tablespoon at a time, till dough begins to clump. Refrigerate.

Meanwhile, toss the apples with sugar, cinnamon, nutmeg, and squeeze lemon over the mixture. Simmer in a saucepan on medium-low heat, stirring occasionally for 15 minutes or until apples are tender.

Roll dough on a lightly floured surface to about 1/8 inch thick. Cut into diamonds about 4 inches by 7 inches. In each center, place 1/4 cup apple filling and fold in half. Press closed with a fork, cut slits in the top, brush with a little egg-white and sprinkle with sugar. Bake at 400 degrees for 12–15 minutes, or until browned.

Yield: 8–10 turnovers.

Above: Left of the turnovers is an easy mulled cider that tastes extraordinary. For 20 minutes, simmer 1 gallon apple cider with 5 teaspoons each of whole cloves and whole allspice in a tea-ball, plus 1 teaspoon ground cinnamon and grated zest of 1 orange. Garnish with cinnamon stick and orange slice.

Sleeping Beauty

Once upon a time, there lived a king and queen who were sad because they had no child. In time they were blessed with a daughter who was as fair as the dawn.

The king held a great feast. Because he had only twelve golden plates, he invited twelve fairies who lived in his kingdom, but a thirteenth fairy was left out.

At the feast, the fairies presented the child with precious and magnificent gifts. One gave her virtue, another beauty, and so on. But as the eleventh fairy finished, the room grew suddenly dark and the thirteenth fairy entered, saying to the king:

A spindle shall pierce thy daughter dear; And death shall end her fifteenth year.

The company gasped and fell silent. The thirteenth fairy disappeared.

Then the twelfth fairy, who had not yet offered her gift, stepped forward and said:

She will not die; But one hundred years asleep shall lie.

That day, the king decreed that all spindles in the kingdom should be burnt.

The princess grew more beautiful with each passing year. Upon her fifteenth birthday, she was seized with a desire to explore an old tower that had not been used for years. She climbed the narrow stairway to the top, and found a small room where an old woman was spinning flax. Fascinated, she reached over to try it herself. As she touched the spindle, it pierced her finger and she fell down in a deep sleep.

Throughout the castle, sleep began to overtake every living thing. A thorn hedge grew higher and higher, surrounding the castle until it could no longer be seen.

Sleeping Beauty's garland in the Star Bedroom, with crystal beads, champagne bows, and white poinsettias. Previous pages, left: Her tree and garland; right: Gilded stars twinkle on the vaulted ceiling above her bed. An oakleaf graces the corner.

any years later, an old man told a young prince from a nearby kingdom the legend of a beautiful princess asleep in a tower that was hidden by thorns. The prince declared he would break the enchantment and free her. The old man warned that he would surely become stuck in the thorns as other princes had, and die.

"I am not afraid of that," said the prince. "I shall go and free the beautiful rose in the briar." The prince took his battle-axe and went to cut through the hedge. But the further he got, the more dense the thorns became. Nor could he go back, because the thorns had grown up again behind him.

He thought to himself, "I may as well go forward, since I might find the princess yet; but if I try to find my way back and fail, we both shall perish." As he reached the spot where the thorns grew so thickly that they obscured the sun, the exact hour passed when one hundred years before, the princess had pricked her finger.

Suddenly, the thorns shrank back and became covered with beautiful blossoms. Before the prince stood an ancient castle. As he came closer, he saw that there were people and animals everywhere, all slumped over in sleep. He walked past the animals, the attendants in the courtyard, and the king and the queen. It was so quiet that he could hear his own breathing.

He came to a tower and climbed the stairs. Inside a room at the top, he saw the princess lying asleep. He was so struck with love for her that he kissed her.

At that moment, the enchantment broke and she awoke. Everyone and everything in the castle was awakened with her, and resumed what it had been doing one hundred years before. The dogs stretched; a fly on the wall started buzzing; the fire flared up; the castle cook turned the roast on the spit; the queen finished what she was saying to the king.

The prince and his lovely "Briar Rose" married and lived in happiness.

Sleepers, Awake

Perhaps Sleeping Beauty will wake up on Christmas morning. Her bed has been draped with a gossamer curtain, and little bows are tied along the length of a bead garland that hangs from the corner.

Below, Sleeping Beauty's first glimpse of her tree—through the curtains of her canopy bed. The misty, dreamlike quality of her room comes from generous amounts of sheer fabric added to the bed's canopy and arranged in cascades from the door frame (pages 64 and 66).

We are such stuff
As dreams are made on,

and our little life
Is rounded with a sleep.
—William Shakespeare

Sleeping Beauty's Breakfast

After the prince introduced himself, Sleeping Beauty's next question was about breakfast. The cook made French toast. It had orange-butter glaze for her, and plenty of eggs in it for the prince.

French Toast

In addition to virtue and beauty, one of the fairies gave Briar Rose a good cook. This recipe works best with a hearty loaf of medium texture. I've had my best results using a gourmet-style "Italian boule" loaf with a light sourdough base, from the local supermarket.

1 20-ounce loaf bread
12 large eggs
1/4 cup each of heavy cream and water
Salt to taste
Olive oil and butter for pan

Cut bread into slices 1/2-inch thick. Cut each slice into 6 to 8 pieces approximately 2 inches square.

In a large bowl, beat eggs lightly with a whisk. Add cream, 1/4 cup water, and salt; blend thoroughly.

In a large skillet, heat 1–2 teaspoons of olive oil and 1/2 teaspoon butter until quite hot.

Meanwhile, soak 8 to 10 pieces of bread in the batter for about 1 minute. Cook until golden brown, turn over, and repeat on second side. Add a small amount of oil and butter for each batch to keep toast from sticking to pan.

Note: This is a forgiving recipe. Instead of 1/4 cup each of cream and water, you can use 3/8 cup fresh-squeezed orange juice or water.

You can also fry the toast in a non-stick pan with less oil and butter. However, the standard butter-and-oil combination creates a pleasantly browned surface.

Yield: about 55 pieces.

Orange-Butter Glaze

1/2 cup unsalted butter, softened
1/2 teaspoon salt
11/3 cups confectioners sugar
2 tablespoons freshly squeezed orange juice
Grated zest of 1 orange

Cream softened butter with salt and 2/3 cup sugar; alternate adding juice with remaining sugar. Add zest. Serve glaze as a topping for the toast in place of butter.

Yield: about 3/4 cup.

*The chocolate "kisses" are made by wrapping purchased truffles in colored foil.
The messages are laser-printed on cotton-fiber bond in a font called Edwardian Script ITC.*

Beauty and the Beast

A rich merchant had three daughters and three sons. One day word came that his fleet of ships had been lost in a storm. The family became poor and moved to a small house in the country.

None of the daughters liked having to do the chores that servants used to do for them, but the youngest daughter, whose name was Beauty, tried not to complain and managed as best she could, as did her brothers. When her work was finished, she amused herself by singing, playing the harpsicord, and reading her beloved books.

The merchant received word that some of his money had been recovered from a ship that arrived safely, so he prepared to make a journey to the far-away port. His older two daughters asked him to bring back fine dresses and jewelry; but when he asked Beauty what she would like, she answered that she would be content with a rose to plant in her garden, for none grew there.

Alas, there was a legal battle over the recovered money, and the merchant had to return home not one bit richer than when he left. While he was about thirty miles away from home, a winter storm arose. He soon lost his way in the snow and rain that fell heavily around him. Afraid he would die in the cold, he suddenly looked up and saw a light through the trees. He followed it to a huge palace that was illuminated from top to bottom.

The merchant entered the gate and saw an open, dry stable. His horse went in and began to eat contentedly, while the merchant himself proceeded to the magnificent hall. A warm fire was burning on the hearth, and before him a table was set for one. He waited for the master of the house to come and eat, but no one came. At eleven o'clock, he sat down and ate. After finishing the meal, he walked through several apartments with the richest furniture. He discovered a bedroom, and since the hour was late and he was tired, he shut the door and went to sleep.

*H*e awoke late the next morning and found that not only was he feeling refreshed, but his worn clothes had been replaced with ones of very good quality, and hot chocolate had been set out for his breakfast. He gave thanks to his unseen host, assuming it must be a fairy, before departing to find his horse. Outside, instead of snow, he saw a garden with arbors and the most beautiful flowers he had ever seen. Remembering Beauty's request, he reached out and plucked a branch that bore several fine roses.

At Beast's castle, Beauty's apartment had a library. The books shown above are from Jay Gould's Cabinet Room—a kind of inner sanctum off his library.

Immediately he heard a deafening roar and saw a truly frightful beast standing before him.

The Beast roared: "I have saved your life by receiving you into my castle, and, in return, you steal my roses, which I value beyond any thing in the universe. For this you shall die."

The merchant begged him for mercy, asking for at least the chance to bid his children farewell. The Beast declared that if one of his daughters should be willing to suffer in his place, the merchant's life would be spared. He was sent on his way, but not empty-handed, for the Beast told him to fill a chest with anything he wished, and he would send it after him.

He arrived at home pale and shaken and gave Beauty the roses. He lamented, "You have little idea how much they have cost me!" and related all that had happened.

His older daughters blamed Beauty for his ill-fortune, but she calmly said "It will not cost our dear father anything, for I will gladly go to the Beast's castle in his place."

"No!" said her brothers, "We will fight the Beast and kill him or die in the attempt."

*B*ut Beauty remained adamant, and no amount of pleading by her father or brothers would change her mind. The next morning, the merchant found the chest he had filled with gold beside his bed. With a heavy heart, he and Beauty set off for the castle. They found no one there, but this time the table was set for two. At the end of their supper, the merchant heard the Beast approach.

He addressed Beauty: "Have you come freely?" She barely stammered a yes in reply.

The Beast turned to the merchant and said: "Honest man, I am greatly obliged to you. Go your way tomorrow morning, but do not try to return here."

Once more the merchant tried to persuade Beauty to go home. But Beauty said, "Leave me to the care and protection of Providence."

While she slept that night, Beauty dreamed a fine lady came and said, "Giving your own life to save your father's shall not go unrewarded." Beauty's father cried bitterly when he took leave of her, though he found some comfort when she told him of the dream.

Now alone, Beauty wandered the halls of the castle, determined to fill the time until evening, when she was sure she would be eaten by the Beast. She came to a door bearing a sign with the words "Beauty's Apartment." She was quite taken with the things inside, which included fine dresses, a library, a harpsicord, and several music books. She opened a book and read these words, written in gold:

Welcome Beauty, banish fear,

You are queen and mistress here.

Speak your wishes, speak your will,

Swift obedience meets them still.

She passed the afternoon, and that evening she sat to dinner. Hearing the Beast approach, she froze in fear. "Beauty," he asked, "may I stay while you eat?"

"If that is your wish," said Beauty.

He insisted, "No, you are mistress here. If you find me troublesome, I will go immediately. Everything here is yours; I will be uneasy if you are not happy. But—do you not find me ugly?"

"Indeed," she replied, "but your kindness so touches me that I scarcely notice your appearance. I prefer it to those whose human shape hides a treacherous and ungrateful heart."

As she finished her dinner, the Beast asked her "Beauty, will you marry me?"

Beauty was frightened to the core once again, but simply said, "No, Beast."

The poor monster sighed, and the hiss was so frightful that the whole palace echoed. He recovered himself and mournfully bid her farewell.

Above and page 71: Beauty's place at Beast's table. The antique plates and crystal echo the details of eighteenth-century French court life described in the tale.

*I*n this way, Beauty passed many months at the palace. She grew more and more fond of the Beast and looked forward to his company, though every evening he asked her the same thing: "Beauty, will you marry me?" And every evening she had to tell him, "No, Beast," for she could not imagine herself as his wife.

The Beast was resigned; he only asked, "Promise me you will never leave."

When she wished to know about her family, Beauty could look in a special mirror and see them as plainly as if they were in the room with her. She saw that her sisters had married men of some importance, and her brothers had gone to the army. Her father was alone and still grieved for her. She asked the Beast if she might go home and see her father, as his sorrow tore at her heart.

The Beast agreed to let her go, saying he would rather die than cause her unhappiness. Beauty promised to return in one week. He told her to take her ring from her finger and lay it on the table beside her when she went to sleep, and in the morning she would find herself at her family's house. At the end of the week, she was to return in the same manner.

She woke up the next morning in the cottage, and her father was so overjoyed that he could not

contain himself. Beauty's sisters came with their husbands, but they were unhappy. One had married an attractive gentleman, and the other had married a man of keen wit, but both husbands were absorbed in themselves and tormented their wives. Seeing Beauty's happiness and the gentle way she had been treated by her Beast was more than they could bear.

All week they showered her with false affection, and when the week ended, they cried and tore their hair, so Beauty agreed to stay another week. They hoped the Beast would grow angry and devour her.

On the tenth night, Beauty dreamed she saw the Beast on the ground in his garden. As he lay dying, he reproached her for her ingratitude. She woke with a start and regretfully thought of her carelessness. "Why did I refuse to marry him? I would be happier with my monster than my sisters are with their husbands."

She took off her ring and placed it on the table beside her. In the morning, she awoke at the palace. She put on the most elegant dress to please her Beast, and waited impatiently for dinner. But the hour came and went, and there was no sign of him. She searched the palace in vain, and then remembered her dream.

She went out into the garden, where she found the Beast on the ground by the stream. She thought he was dead, and fell upon him sobbing. But though he lay still, his heart was beating, so Beauty brought some water to cool his face.

The Beast opened his eyes and said, "You forgot your promise, and I could no longer eat. But since I have the happiness of seeing you once more, I die content."

"Oh, Beast!" she sobbed, "Please live, and be my husband! From this moment I give you my hand. I thought I had but friendship for you, but I cannot live without you."

Beauty and Beast's tree in the Cabinet Room at Lyndhurst: gold for Beauty; royal purple for Beast. The bows recall the fine gown she wore on the night she agreed to be his wife.

No sooner had these words been spoken when the whole palace sparkled with light, and beautiful music filled the air. Before Beauty stood a noble prince who would have commanded anyone's attention. But Beauty only saw that her Beast had disappeared, and sadly asked the prince where he was.

"You behold him," he said. "I was condemned by a curse to live as a Beast until an honorable maiden should freely consent to marry me. Though I offer you my crown, it will not repay the debt I owe you." He held out his hand to her, and they walked to the palace.

They were greeted in the palace by the same beautiful woman who had appeared to Beauty in her dream. She said to Beauty: "Come and receive your reward. You have preferred virtue before wit or beauty. You merit someone in whom all these qualities are united. You shall be a great queen."

Beauty's father and family came, though her sisters were not allowed to enter the palace until they had admitted their guilt and repented of their envy and maliciousness.

In an instant, the company was transported to the prince's kingdom, where his subjects received him with joy. He married Beauty and lived with her many long years. Their happiness—being founded on virtue—was complete.

Beauty is everywhere a welcome guest.
—Johann Wolfgang von Goethe

Right, and page 70: Details of Beauty and the Beast's tree in the Dining Room at Lyndhurst, showing the golden pears and twisted icicle ornaments.

Opposite: Instead of randomly mixing the ornaments, the purple ones have been wired onto a matching tinsel garland, so they hang in the same scalloped pattern, clearly visible from a distance. The amber and gold ornaments fill out the rest of the tree. This tree has still more impact because of the large-scale ornaments used throughout, especially near the bottom.

Beauty and the Beef

Roast beef was served at Christmas dinner in Europe for hundreds of years before Columbus saw his first turkey. Using this chef's trick, you'll discover why.

Tenderloin of Beef

Our friend Mark Kaplan, a chef, says cooking filet mignon is more art than science. But many of the tricks of the chef trade are not hard to learn. Start with the right spices, and seal in the flavor:

131/2-pound beef tenderloin
Kosher salt
Freshly ground pepper
Granulated garlic powder
Dried thyme
Olive oil

Trim off fat and carefully peel the "silver" skin from the tenderloin. Sprinkle with kosher salt, pepper, a light coating of garlic powder, thyme, and olive oil. Brown in a skillet. (Cut tenderloin into two shorter filets if too long.)

Cook in a roasting pan at 425 degrees for about 25 minutes. If you're using a meat thermometer, check the smaller piece (the tail portion) first. The temperature in the thickest part of it should read 110 degrees for rare, 120 degrees for medium. The second filet will take 5 to 10 minutes longer.

Yield: about 30 generous portions.

Texas Hand Test: Once you get the feel of it, the following method for judging the doneness of meat is at least as reliable as piercing it with a thermometer—and it won't let juices escape and dry out the meat.

Your right hand is the "meat," and your left hand is the tester: Hold your right hand palm-up and bring your thumb and your index finger together so they barely touch. With your left hand, feel the part of your palm just below the thumb joint. Then feel your cooking roast. If they feel the same, the meat is rare.

For medium, touch the thumb to the middle finger and feel the same place on your palm.

Touch the thumb to the pinky for well done.

Above: Filet mignon served with slices of focaccia next to a carving fork ornamented with a stag.
Opposite, above: A mantelpiece garland in Beast's dining room; below: Beast's place at the table.

The Princess and the Pea

How do you tell if a princess is real?

A prince wanted to marry, so he traveled all over the world to find a princess. Though he met many fair girls who claimed to be princesses, none of them truly was.

The prince was sad. Being a somewhat picky young man, he wanted to marry someone just as particular as he.

One evening during a terrible storm, a young lady showed up at the city gate. She claimed to be a princess, but she was so bedraggled that no one could tell for sure. Why, just look at her! Water was running in and out of her shoes, and she was soaked through and through from the torrential rain.

So the old Queen (the prince's mother) devised a test. She put a pea underneath a mattress. On top of that she ordered the servants to lay nineteen more mattresses, and on top of those, twenty feather beds. The young woman was led in to sleep on this bed for the night.

The next morning she was asked how she slept: "Oh, very badly!" she replied without hesitation. She explained that she lay awake most of the night, because there was something so hard under her mattress that it bruised her all over!

Now the prince was very happy indeed, because he knew that she was a real princess. No one else could have felt a pea under twenty mattresses and twenty feather beds. So he married her right away!

And the pea? That was put in a museum where you can still see it, if no one has stolen it.

Here you see the princess's bed piled high with mattresses.

Opposite: The prince's family has generously provided her with a ladder so that she can get to the top. The princess's crown is on the chair beside the bed—of course, crowns are too prickly to wear while sleeping. (If a pea is enough to bruise her all over, imagine the damage a crown could do!)

Here are sweet peas on tip-toe for a flight,
With wings of gentle flush o'er delicate white,
And taper fingers catching at all things,
To bind them all about with tiny rings.
—John Keats

Magnetic Inspiration?

Hans Christian Andersen seemed to draw inspiration from almost anything that touched him, from a scrap of paper trash *(Auntie Toothache)* to the garden of the Chinese Emperor *(The Nightingale)*. He prided himself on the wit and inside jokes he wove into his stories for the amusement of the adults he knew would be listening. It is well known that *The Nightingale* is a tribute to a friend, the singer Jenny Lind.

I have often wondered if Andersen wrote *The Princess and the Pea* with a little something extra in mind. It has the style of a lighthearted allusion—in addition to being an endearing homage to picky princesses and the picky men who love them.

A bachelor all his life, Andersen was a regular dinner guest at the houses of many of Copenhagen's brightest stars in theater, art, and science, where he would entertain the company with his paper cuttings and story telling. Those who had the good fortune to hear him have described the effect as mesmerizing.

One of the homes he frequented for dinner was that of Hans Christian Oersted, his former philosophy professor at the University of Copenhagen. Both Andersen and Oersted were keenly interested in the arts, philosophy, and science, and often discussed the implications of new scientific discoveries. Oersted was famous as the discoverer of electromagnetism (the relationship between electricity and magnetic force) in 1820.

In 1835, Andersen published his first novel, *The Improvisatore*, which was an instant success. The same year, he wrote and published *The Princess and the Pea* with three other stories in a tiny volume of fairy tales. Upon reading them, Oersted exclaimed, "If the novel has made you famous, the fairy tale will make you immortal!"

Curiously, 1835 was also the year in which Samuel F.B. Morse created a working model of the electronic telegraph, and proved that it could be a viable way to communicate over long distances.

Morse's device used Oersted's discovery, electromagnetism, to transmit a tiny little bit of information invisibly to a receiver some distance away, which would then register the information. In the fairy tale, the Princess is able to feel the effects of the pea through forty layers of fluff (twenty mattresses and twenty eiderdown quilts).

And the distance Morse's first telegraph was able to send its message? Forty feet.

Making Pillow Ornaments

These silk shantung "ornaments" were not ornaments to begin with, but sachets purchased at a sample sale—that just happen to look like tiny pillows or mattresses.

The sachets are made from 3½-inch squares of silk shantung, sewn with a 1/4-inch seam allowance. If you want to make your own, you can also try other opulent fabrics such as small-scale brocades or Indian sari cloth. Don't forget to leave a little opening for turning them right side out and stuffing them.

Above: To finish your sachets, tie them in bundles of three with a ribbon. These have beads sewn to the corners and top, but they'd look just as beautiful with almost any simple decoration. Use Fabri-tac glue for keeping wayward bits of ribbon or other small decorations in place. (See pattern, page 156.)

Adding dried lavender and hops to the stuffing (but not peas!) will help the Princess sleep more peacefully from now on.

Opposite: The Princess's tree in the North Bedroom at Lyndhurst. The ornamentation on the ceiling reflects the Romantic style. Many of the European furnishings were collected by Jay Gould's daughter Anna, Duchess of Talleyrand-Perigord, who lived in the room growing up and stayed there when she visited the house.

If I Were Two Inches Tall...

I'd love to hang out on this tree. There's a house to live in, pillows to lounge on, and peas to eat.

Above: A detail of the crystal garlands on the Princess's tree. Two strands hung side-by-side reflect light like a chandelier and give a more opulent look.

Left: Fantasy themes like The Princess and the Pea offer countless possibilities for variation and humor. We expect shiny ornaments to be made of fragile glass—but these are soft and puffy.

Right: Tiny pink balls dance next to a pea-pod ornament. They are so small that they would disappear underneath the branches if they were hung individually with standard ornament hangers. Instead, they are wired on in little clusters, so they look as if they just bounced there.

Princess Peas

These peas are guaranteed to please even the pickiest princess.
I say this with confidence because I have observed them to magically
disappear from the bowl before they even made it to the banquet hall.

Princess Peas

Olive oil to coat pan
1 teaspoon unsalted butter
1/2 teaspoon salt
1/2 teaspoon dried garlic flakes
1 cup frozen petite peas

Heat the oil in a skillet on medium heat. Melt the butter, add salt and garlic flakes, and heat slightly. Add frozen peas (do not thaw first) and sauté for a minute or two.

Cook until just-past-thawed, so the peas are slightly crisp, with a light burst of flavor.

Peas on a Pillow

Though excellent by themselves, Princess Peas can be served with softened chevre (goat cheese) as a topping—shown on a bed of food-grade rose petals. Take heed: They may disappear even faster, since the sweetness of the peas and the tartness of the cheese seem to bring out the best qualities of both.

Yield: 2–4 servings.

Other good companions for Princess Peas include crackers, salad, or thin slices of baguette.

The Princess's crown is from a teen accessory store. A jewel "pea"
is a green glass bead, attached to the center with bead wire.

The Little Mermaid

On their fifteenth birthdays, mermaid princesses are allowed to go up to the ocean surface for the first time and see the world above the water.

The Little Mermaid was the youngest and prettiest daughter of the Sea King. For years, she dreamed about what that other world would be like. Finally, her turn came. As she rose to the surface, a beautiful sunset revealed a sailing ship where a prince was celebrating his sixteenth birthday. The ship was hung with colored lanterns, and there was music, singing, and grand fireworks.

Then a terrible storm arose. The ship capsized, but the Mermaid was able to save the prince's life and carry him to safety on the beach, where a group of young maidens found him. As she returned home to the depths, the Mermaid could think of nothing but the prince and his world beyond the sea. Everything she treasured—her coral reef garden, her freedom, her beautiful voice— now paled before her love for the prince and her enchantment with mankind.

The Little Mermaid's wise grandmother explained to her that land people have short lives, unlike mermaids, who can live three hundred years before they turn into sea-foam. But each human being has a soul that lives forever. The sea princess longed to have a soul. Her grandmother told her that if a man loved her enough to marry her, she could share his soul and someday go to heaven.

A treasure chest spills over with pearls and bubbles. Previous pages, left: The Little Mermaid's dressing table; right: Her "blue bubble" tree.

etermined to win the prince for her husband and gain a soul, the Little Mermaid went to the evil sea-witch for help. The witch, who lived in a house built with the bones of shipwrecked human beings, offered the Mermaid a glittering, poisonous drink that would turn her fish's tail into legs and let her walk on dry land. For this, she would have to trade her beautiful voice. The witch also warned her that walking would be very painful, and that if the prince married someone else, the Mermaid's heart would break, and she would die at dawn on the morning after the wedding.

At nightfall, the Mermaid swam to the steps of the prince's palace at the edge of the sea and drank the potion. It was so awful, she fainted. The prince himself found her on the beach and took her to the palace. She captured the heart of everyone at court with her beautiful, expressive eyes and ethereal dancing. But she could neither sing nor talk, and every step caused her terrible pain.

The prince grew very fond of her. She accompanied him on horseback journeys, and was given permission to sleep at his door on a velvet cushion. One day he confided to her that the only girl he would marry was one who had saved his life after a shipwreck, and that the Mermaid resembled her. But the prince did not remember being carried to the beach. He thought he had been saved by one of the maidens who found him. He didn't recognize that his rescuer was the mute girl before him!

As time went on, the prince was told he must marry a certain princess from a neighboring kingdom. As it happened, the princess was the girl he thought had saved him. A grand wedding was planned.

The evening after the wedding, the prince's party retired to a ship to celebrate. With a broken heart, the poor Mermaid sat at the helm of the ship, waiting for the sun to rise and bring her death.

Out of the water, the Mermaid's sisters appeared. Their long, beautiful hair was cut off: They had traded it to the sea-witch for a chance to save her life. The witch gave them a knife for the Mermaid; if she plunged it into the prince's heart while he slept, she could save herself and return to the sea.

But the Little Mermaid's love for her prince was true. Trembling and resigned to her fate, she flung the sea-witch's dagger into the sea as the sun rose, and then threw herself into the waves.

Instead of dying, the Mermaid suddenly found herself lifted into the mist and surrounded by air-spirits. They told her that because of her sacrifice, she had become a daughter of the air like them. They carry breezes around the earth to bring fresh air and the perfume of flowers to people everywhere, and visit houses where there are good children. By doing good works, air spirits can earn a soul.

The spirits promised the Mermaid that she would go to paradise with them when their work on earth was accomplished, to live with the sons and daughters of mankind forever.

Unseen by anyone aboard the ship, the Little Mermaid fanned the prince, kissed the forehead of his bride, and floated with the other children of the air to a rosy cloud that soared high above the earth.

Bring a Deep-Sea World to Life

Since she will be hanging around earth for a few hundred years before she gets to heaven, the Little Mermaid has taken over the bathroom at Lyndhurst, where she has a bath and dressing mirror very much like her underwater ones. She has given the room her deep-sea look.

Unusual lighting gives the bathroom its underwater glow. Bubbles seem to froth up and spill out from the bathtub and sink, but here's what's going on under the surface.

In the bathtub (pages 96–97), the bubbles are medium-size, clear glass Christmas balls with the caps and hangers removed. They sit on top of a cardboard box, mini-lights, and bubble-wrap. The box is there to take up extra space in the middle of the tub (otherwise there would have to be about twice as many bubbles!) and also to provide a platform for the lights. Here's how the items in the tub are put together to achieve the effect:

The cardboard box goes in first, in the middle of the tub; then a layer of 1/8-inch foam packing sheet is very loosely laid on top like a blanket.

On top of the foam is a string of white mini-lights, laid randomly. Over the lights is a layer of large bubble-wrap, and finally the glass ball "bubbles," placed with the necks down.

Bubbles and fish ornaments have been looped onto the twigs of a driftwood branch to give them the illusion of floating there. The branch itself is held in place by more bubbles in the sink. Collections of little shells, a natural sponge, and other reminders of the deep sea all help the Little Mermaid feel more at home.

The marble double-sink (page 88) contains a simpler bubble-bath: A string of mini-lights with glass balls on top fills the closest basin. The far one hides a white "can light" aimed upward to illuminate the garland over the mirror. Draping the countertop is a blue net with little shells scattered around the edges.

Four-inch aqua and 2 1/2-inch, royal blue silk ribbons add the final flourish.

Glass fish ornaments "swim" from the garlands over the sink and the bathtub. Suspended invisibly from nylon fishing line, they twirl with the slightest movement of air. Nylon line also attaches one end of the net above the sink to the shower-curtain rod a few feet away, creating a canopy over the sink.

Filled with a wonderful glass-bubble "topiary," the compote on the sink is a light-hearted twist on the traditional fruit versions. Glass balls stacked up in a pyramid fashion are hot-glued to each other—but not to the bowl—so the entire unit can be removed and packed away. The balls that fill the bottom of the bowl are glued to each other first; the next layer is hot-glued to the previous one, and so on all the way up, decreasing the number of balls as they go. It is completed by grape floral picks and seashells glued around the sides. It's illuminated by the can light in the sink behind it.

In the Underwater Suite…

The Mermaid's dressing mirror is the height
of ocean-floor fashion, with garlands of pearls,
an artificial pine swag, tinsel, a starfish or
two, and a canopy made
from fishermen's net.

Nylon fishing line is used to secure the pine swag to three screw eyes along the top of the mirror frame in back. The nylon line is used instead of florists' wire since it is less likely to damage the surface of valuable or antique items. Pearls, ribbons, tinsel garland, net canopy, and other ornaments are then wired directly onto the pine swag. Some glass balls with the caps removed are stuck onto a few pine branches.

Left: Even mermaids need bathtubs. The curtain is made from three layers of sheer blue and green fabric. It is cut in large scallops and hemmed. The fish and bubble ornaments are suspended invisibly from nylon fishing line so that they "swim" from the garlands over the sink and the bathtub—swaying and turning on tiny currents of air in the room.

Previous two pages: Detail of the Little Mermaid's sink. Mini-lights secreted in the sink underneath the glass-ornament "bubbles" give the whole fixture an unearthly glow.

Above: A bow made from four-inch-wide aqua silk ribbon with royal blue accents—fit for a sea-king's daughter. Left: Detail of the bathtub and its idly swimming fish. Below: Barely visible under the clear glass balls is a string of white mini-lights.

> We are as near to heaven
> by sea as by land.
> —Sir Humphrey Gilbert

Hors d'oeuvres served on seashells. The most intriguing shells have richly colored or iridescent, mother-of-pearl interiors. Even a simple crafts-store purchase, like this abalone (right, and above at left), makes a charming little serving dish.

Little Mermaid's Seafood Delicacies

On Christmas Eve, many nations have a tradition of not eating meat
until after Midnight Mass: They serve as many as 12 different seafood dishes.
When they're appetizer portions like these, you have room to enjoy them all.

Mini-Pizzas with Anchovies

*The Little Mermaid has grown to love
land food, especially pizza (she is a teenager,
after all). She likes hers with anchovies. Even
non-mermaids can get hooked on these.*

Making Basic Tomato Sauce:

1–2 tablespoons of regular or garlic-
 infused olive oil
2 (6-ounce) cans tomato paste
 (I use Contadina original style, no herbs)
1 (28-ounce) can whole peeled
 tomatoes in puree (Redpack)
About 20 large basil leaves (or five tops)

Heat oil in pan. Add tomato paste and
heat lightly, then whole tomatoes, chopped
up. Bring to a slight boil, then reduce
heat and simmer for about 1 1/4 hours.

Tear up the basil leaves and add to the
sauce; heat for another 10 minutes.

Assembling the Pizzas:

Tomato sauce (see recipe above)
20 mini-pita breads sliced in half and
 toasted—or similar small-size toast
1 pound fresh mozzarella, thinly sliced
5 tins of rolled anchovies with capers
Olive oil
40 small leaves of fresh basil

Lay toasted bread slices face up on a foil-
covered cookie sheet and spread a spoonful of
sauce on each one. Add a slice of mozzarella,
a rolled anchovy, and drizzle a little olive oil
(or oil from the anchovies) over the top.

Heat in an oven set at 350 degrees for
7–10 minutes, or under a broiler for 2–5
minutes. WATCH CAREFULLY and remove
them just after the cheese melts. Add a small
basil leaf to the top of each pizza and serve.

Yield: 40 mini-pizzas.

Smoked Salmon Appetizer

40 small slices of bread such as pumper-
 nickel, bagel, or baguette
1/4 cup butter
1 pound smoked salmon
16-ounce container of sour cream
3–5 tomatoes, or a 12-ounce
 container of grape tomatoes, sliced
1/4 cup chives, cut into 1/4-inch pieces
1/4 cup capers for garnish
1 cucumber, diced

Toast and butter the bread slices,
then add a small piece of smoked salmon
with a dollop of sour cream and a slice
of tomato to each. Garnish with chives,
capers, and cucumber, if desired.

Yield: 40 appetizers.

Alice's Adventures in Wonderland

Alice was beginning to get very tired of sitting by her sister on the bank of the river on a hot day with nothing to do—when suddenly, a White Rabbit with pink eyes ran close by her.

It seemed quite natural that the Rabbit was saying to itself, "Oh dear! Oh dear! I shall be too late!" But then, it took a watch out of its waistcoat-pocket, looked at it, and hurried on. Burning with curiosity, Alice ran after it and followed it down a large rabbit-hole under the hedge.

Thump! thump! Alice came to rest upon a heap of sticks and dry leaves. She found herself in a long, low hall, and came upon a little three-legged table made of glass. On it was a tiny golden key.

In the hallway was a door about fifteen inches high. She tried the key in the lock, and the door opened into the loveliest enclosed garden you ever saw. How she longed to wander about among those beds of bright flowers and cool fountains! But she could not even get her head through the doorway.

On the table she found a little bottle (which wasn't there before). It had a paper label with the words "DRINK ME," beautifully printed in large letters. Seeing that the bottle was not marked "poison" anywhere, she ventured to taste it. She found it very nice, and soon finished it off.

Alice felt herself getting smaller—until she was only ten inches high, just the right size for entering the garden. But alas! She had forgotten the key on the glass table, now too high for her to reach.

She began to cry, and was just berating herself for it when her eye fell upon a little glass box. Inside was a very small cake, on which the words "EAT ME" were beautifully marked in currants.

"Well, I'll eat it," said Alice. "If it makes me grow larger, I can reach the key; and if it makes me grow smaller, I can creep under the door!" She grew swiftly until she was nine feet tall. Now Alice could barely fit one eye in front of the doorway of the garden to look in! She began to cry again.

Alice shed gallons of tears, until there was a large pool all round her about four inches deep. As she cried, she began fanning herself with a fan the White Rabbit had dropped.

She soon discovered that fanning herself was making her shrink rapidly. She dropped the fan hastily when she saw that she was a few inches high, and made her way out of doors and into a thick wood.

She came in sight of a house with chimneys shaped like ears and a roof thatched with fur. The March Hare (for it was his house) and the Mad Hatter were seated at a table under a tree, having a tea party. A Dormouse was sitting between them, fast asleep. The table was large, and the three were all crowded together at one corner.

"No room! No room!" they cried out when they saw Alice coming.

"There's *plenty* of room!" said Alice indignantly, and she sat down at the end in a large arm-chair.

"Have some wine," the March Hare said in an encouraging tone.

"I don't see any wine," she remarked.

"There isn't any," said the March Hare.

"Then it wasn't very civil of you to offer it," said Alice angrily.

"It wasn't very civil of you to sit down without being invited."

"I didn't know it was your table," said Alice. "It's laid for a great many more than three."

"Your hair wants cutting," said the Hatter. He had been looking at Alice for some time with great curiosity, and this was his first speech.

"You should learn not to make personal remarks," Alice said with some severity. "It's very rude." When she left the table, Alice saw that the Mad Hatter and the March Hare were trying to stuff the sleeping Dormouse into the teapot.

Picking her way through the wood, she came upon a tree with a door leading right into it. She opened it, and once more found herself in the hall by the little glass table. She picked up the little golden key and unlocked the door to the garden. And *then*—she found herself at last among the bright flower-beds and the cool fountains. A large rose-tree stood near the entrance. The roses growing on it were white, but three gardeners were busily painting them red. The gardeners had regular heads and limbs, but their bodies were numbered playing-cards.

"Would you tell me," asked Alice, a little timidly, "why you are painting those roses?"

Five and Seven looked at Two. Two began in a low voice, "Why the fact is, Miss, this here ought to have been a red rose-tree, and we put a white one in by mistake. If the Queen was to find it out, we should all have our heads cut off—"

At this moment Five, who had been anxiously peering across the garden, called out "The Queen!"

The King and Queen of Hearts had arrived, with an entourage of clubs, spades, and diamonds.

The Queen demanded that the company play a most unusual game of croquet. The balls were hedgehogs, and the mallets flamingoes. The chief difficulty Alice found was in managing her flamingo. She got its body tucked away under her arm with its legs hanging down, but just as she had got its neck straightened out and was going to give the hedgehog a blow with the head, it *would* twist itself round and look up into her face with such a puzzled expression that she could not help bursting out laughing. When she had got its head down and was ready to begin again, it was very provoking to find that the hedgehog had unrolled itself and was crawling away.

A large, grinning Cheshire Cat appeared in the air nearby, with only its head visible. Alice had met it earlier. She was giving it an account of the game when the King approached. After the Cat declined to kiss his ring, the Queen cried, "Off with its head!" But the executioner protested that you couldn't cut off a head unless there was a body to cut it off *from*.

The Queen declared herself winner of the game. The whole party left for the the trial of the Knave of Hearts, to be presided over by the King. In the court, the White Rabbit read the charge:

The Queen of Hearts, she made some tarts, all on a summer's day. The Knave of Hearts, he stole those tarts and took them quite away.

Alice, who was growing again, was called to testify. As she got up, the edge of her skirt brushed against the jury box, spilling out all the jurymen. "Oh, I beg your pardon!" she said, putting them back.

Asked what she knew of the crime, Alice said "Nothing."

"That's very important," the King said, turning to the jury. Then he added, "Let the jury consider their verdict."

"No, no!" said the Queen. "Sentence first—verdict afterwards."

"Stuff and nonsense!" said Alice loudly.

"Hold your tongue!" said the Queen, turning purple.

"I won't!" said Alice.

"Off with her head!" the Queen shouted. Nobody moved.

"Who cares for you?" said Alice (who had grown to her full size by this time). "You're nothing but a pack of cards!"

At this, the whole pack rose up into the air and came flying down upon her. She gave a little scream and tried to beat them off. She found herself lying on the river bank. Her head was in the lap of her sister, who was gently brushing away some leaves that had fluttered from the trees onto her face.

Alice said, "Oh, I've had such a curious dream!"

Above and page 100: Pink, plastic lawn flamingoes!

The Perils of Poetry

Alice and her adventures in Wonderland first came to life when a young mathematics lecturer sat in a boat one summer day, improvising a story to amuse a friend and the three young daughters of his dean at Oxford. The lecturer's name was Rev. Charles Lutwidge Dodgson. Reversing the order of his first and middle names, he created the pen-name "Lewis Carroll" and published *Alice's Adventures in Wonderland* three years later in late 1865. It quickly became a worldwide best-seller.

In the story, Alice finds herself in a dreamlike world of adult maniacs. She out-wits and overcomes them by refusing to be trifled with—but makes heroic efforts to maintain her good will and good manners. Periodically, she tries to dispel the confusion around her by reminding herself who she is and what she knows—such as the poems she regularly recites for her lessons. These verses, many of them rather patronizing and didactic, were known to most school-age English children in the 1860s. Throughout the book, eight such poems serve as targets for Dodgson's wit.

Having become a nine-foot-high giantess trapped in an uncomfortable position in the hallway at the bottom of a rabbit burrow, Alice reassures herself by crossing her hands neatly in her lap and reciting what she hopes will be the first two stanzas of "Against Idleness and Mischief," by the famous writer of hymns, Isaac Watts (1674–1748). But her hope is in vain. In Wonderland, the words of poems are no more constant than one's height. Watts's poem begins:

How doth the little busy bee
Improve each shining hour.
And gather honey all the day
From every opening flower!

How skillfully she builds her cell!
How neat she spreads the wax!

Above and right: Many ornaments are made from playing cards and from Alice-themed greeting cards.

And labours hard to store it well
With the sweet food she makes.

But that isn't the way Alice recites it. Here is her version:

How doth the little crocodile
Improve his shining tail,
And pour the waters of the Nile
On every golden scale!

How cheerfully he seems to grin,
How neatly spread his claws,
And welcome little fishes in
With gently smiling jaws!

After Alice shrinks to three inches high and escapes the house, she seeks a caterpillar's advice. When she describes her recent memory problems, he has her recite a famous poem by Robert Southey (1774–1843)—the uncle of Dodgson's lifelong friend Reginald Southey. It begins:

"You are old, father William,"
the young man cried, "The few locks
which are left you are grey;
You are hale, father William, a hearty old man;
Now tell me the reason, I pray."

"In the days of my youth," father William replied,
"I remember'd that youth would fly fast,
And Abus'd not my health and my vigour at first,
That I never might need them at last."

But poor Alice comes out with this:

"You are old, Father William," the young man said,
"And your hair has become very white;
And yet you incessantly stand on your head—
Do you think, at your age, it is right?"

"In my youth," Father William replied to his son,
"I feared it might injure the brain;
But, now that I'm perfectly sure I have none,
Why, I do it again and again."

When she got to the end, Alice said timidly, "Not quite right, I'm afraid."

"It is wrong from beginning to end," said the Caterpillar decidedly.

Above: A swirled detail from the ceiling in the Library looks very much like the ribbon roses on Alice's tree.

Left: The ribbon roses themselves (a crimson one is visible near the bottom of the photo) are made by rolling up the ribbon while bunching it slightly at the base, and then winding the base with floral wire.

Far left: The rose tree was made from a silk rose garland that was hot-glued to a green bamboo garden stake. The stake is mounted in a planter for stability.

Top: Each end of the garland over the window is given a flourish inspired by the Cheshire Cat: three huge, striped globes that hang from ribbons.

For tips on making the playing-card garland and laying temporary flooring, see "Making Magic," page 152.

White Rabbit's Carrot Cake

I've tinkered with the chemistry of this cake for ages, but it still works only one way: While it definitely can make me grow larger, I can't get it to work the other way, no matter how much I eat.

White Rabbit's Carrot Cake

This is a variation on a Victorian applesauce cake. For this cake, I use three Wilton mini fluted tube pans.

1 cup flour
1/3 cup sugar
3/4 teaspoon baking soda
3/4 teaspoon salt
1 tablespoon cocoa powder
1/4 teaspoon each of cinnamon, cloves, nutmeg, and allspice
1/4 cup (1/2 stick) unsalted butter, softened
3/4 cup canned carrots, mashed
1 egg
3/8 cup each of chopped golden raisins, dates, and pecans

Mix flour, sugar, soda, salt, cocoa, and spices together in a bowl. Cut in butter; add mashed carrots and beat at low speed or by hand until mixed. Add egg and beat once more. Add dried fruit and nuts and mix thoroughly.

Pour into 3 mini tube pans and bake 30 to 35 minutes at 350 degrees. Done when toothpick inserted in thickest part comes out clean.

Yield: 3 mini-cakes (about 9 servings).

Buttercream Frosting:

1 stick salted butter, softened
1 teaspoon vanilla extract
2 cups confectioners sugar
2 tablespoons heavy cream
Currants for decoration

Mix butter with vanilla and 1 cup sugar. Alternate adding remaining sugar and cream till icing is of spreading consistency. Ice the cakes, pipe a border around the bottom and top, and letter "EAT ME" in currants with a tweezer.

Above: The cake is served on a pink trellis plate from a vintage mold by the L. E. Smith company.

Peter Pan

This is a synopsis of the play by James Matthew Barrie that brought Peter Pan into the world. It opened in London on December 27, 1904, and was called Peter Pan, or The Boy Who Wouldn't Grow Up.

On the day he was born, Peter Pan overheard his parents discussing his future. Not wanting to grow up, he ran away from home so that he could remain a boy forever.

A young girl named Wendy Darling lives with her parents and two younger brothers, John and Michael, in a house in London. The Darlings' life is fairly typical except for the fact that instead of a nursemaid for the children, they have a prim Newfoundland dog named Nana. She wears a nurse-maid's cap and performs all a nursemaid's usual duties, including making the beds and having the children take their medicine—which is always a difficult act of persuasion.

One evening, as their parents are preparing to go out, the boys' antics lead to some household chaos. Mr. Darling tries to convince Michael, the youngest, to take his medicine by volunteering to take his at the same time—but Mr. Darling puts his own medicine into Nana's dish instead. Nana won't drink it, and to the dismay of the children, he unjustly banishes her to the doghouse outside.

Mrs. Darling is nervous about separating Nana from the children because she recently has seen a small boy prowling in the nursery. She shows Mr. Darling the shadow the boy left behind as he escaped out the window just as she was shutting it.

Later that night while her parents are still out, Wendy awakes and is shocked to find the boy, Peter Pan, sneaking about the nursery looking for his lost shadow. He is accompanied by a fist-sized ball of light, which is revealed to be a pixie named Tinkerbell. While Wendy generously sews his shadow back on, Peter tells her that he has often come by to listen to her mother tell the children stories, such as "Cinderella." To Tinkerbell's jealous horror, Wendy is completely charmed by Peter.

Peter convinces Wendy to come with him to his island, called Neverland, so that she can be mother to his scruffy band of followers, known as the "Lost Boys." Peter teaches all the Darling children to fly so that they can make the trip, too. As they approach the island, envious Tinkerbell tricks the witless Lost Boys into shooting at Wendy. She falls from the sky. Though weakened by her injuries, Wendy recovers. Peter commands the boys to build her a house so she can rest. They ask her what kind of house she wants. She tells them:

I wish I had a woodland house,

The littlest ever seen,

With funny little red walls

And roof of mossy green.

In addition, Neverland is fraught with other dangers: The beautiful mermaids are jealous and spiteful, and the pirates led by bloodthirsty Captain Hook are determined to kill just about everybody. Hook has sworn particular revenge on Peter, since Peter cut off Hook's hand in a fight and threw it to a crocodile.

That same crocodile now follows Hook wherever he goes, hoping to eat the rest of him. But the croc has also swallowed a clock, which remains inside him and makes a loud "tick-tock" noise, which warns (and terrifies) Hook whenever it approaches.

One day the children go to a rock in the mermaids' lagoon, hoping to catch a mermaid. The sky darkens and Hook and his men approach with a captive Indian princess, Tiger Lily. The pirates are intending to leave Tiger Lily tied to a rock so that she drowns as the tide comes in. Peter tricks Hook's men into letting Tiger Lily go, and engages Hook in a fight. Hook escapes, Peter is wounded, and he and Wendy are left stranded on the rock. Peter puts Wendy on a kite so that she can fly to safety, and he escapes on a nest floated to him by one of the island's huge native birds, called Never birds. He uses his shirt as a sail.

Back at Peter's house under the ground, he and Wendy act as parents to the Lost Boys. In the midst of telling them a story one evening, Wendy suddenly realizes how grief-stricken her own mother must be, and she resolves to return home with her brothers. She convinces the Lost Boys to come with them so they can be cared for by her mother. Peter prefers to stay behind—because he does not want to leave Neverland and grow up.

On the ground above them, they hear the clamor of a battle between the pirates and the Indians. All becomes quiet. When they hear the tom-tom, they conclude that the victory has gone to their allies, the Indians. Wendy and the rest of the group prepare to depart for London, and she reminds Peter to take his medicine.

As the children emerge, one by one, from Peter's underground hideout, they are captured by the stealthy pirates—who had actually won the battle. The pirates have sat quietly, waiting to snare the children. Then Hook sneaks down into Peter's hideout to pour poison into his medicine. Peter prepares to drink it, but Tinkerbell warns him not to.

Peter thinks Tinkerbell is simply acting jealous of Wendy again, doesn't believe her, and starts to drink. In desperation, Tinkerbell drinks the poison herself. Her fairy-glow begins to fade. As it does, Peter sees that she is dying. At wit's end, he turns to the audience and asks everyone to help bring Tinkerbell back to life by clapping—to show they believe in fairies. The audience (always) responds, Tinkerbell revives, and Peter goes off to save the others.

The children have been taken to Hook's pirate ship, the *Jolly Roger,* and told that they will walk the plank. As Wendy is encouraging them to die like gentlemen, everyone suddenly hears an approaching "tick-tock." The

Above and opposite: Peter's tree in the Library. Page 109: The crocodile (in the Northwest Bedroom) is a party mask.

children have seen the source of the ticking noise, and it isn't the crocodile. It's Peter. But the pirates don't know this.

Panic overtakes the pirate crew, as one after another deserts the ship in terror. Peter and Hook battle once again. As Hook sees his chances of winning fade, he tries to blow up the ship. When Peter stops him, the defeated Hook jumps overboard—where the real crocodile is there to greet him.

Back in London, Mrs. Darling is playing the piano. She has been waiting mournfully for her children to return, but without much hope. Mr. Darling has taken up residence in the children's room, in Nana's doghouse.

The children surprise their mother by sneaking back into their beds and hiding under the covers. At first she doesn't believe her eyes. Peter hovers with Tinkerbell outside—he doesn't want Wendy to stay in London. Wendy asks her mother if she can go back to Neverland, because he needs a mother.

Mrs. Darling firmly tells Wendy no: Wendy needs a mother, too. She hugs her daughter for dear life. But she agrees that Wendy can go back to Neverland once a year to do Peter's spring cleaning for him.

The final scene is in Wendy's little tree-top house in Neverland on a spring evening. The daylight has faded and the fairies are glowing like little fireflies in the surrounding trees. Wendy and Peter are sitting on the porch and the curtain of night falls to the sound of Peter's pan-pipes.

Peter Pan's colors are lime and emerald-green: He is named after Pan, the Greek god of the woods. Here, in a twist on the traditional Christmas colors, red is used sparingly as an accent, so that it doesn't compete with the green—which

is used in several shades. The dark green balls that look like crocodile hide are inexpensive plastic ornaments that were just the right color. *Overleaf: Peter Pan's tree in the Northwest Bedroom is divided vertically with green ribbons. All the bows are simply loops wound with florist's wire.*

When I was ten, I read fairy tales in secret, and would have been ashamed if I had been found doing so. Now that I am 50, I read them openly.

—C. S. Lewis

Crocodile Tears Punch

In Neverland, the food can be real or imaginary. (Before Wendy got there, it was all the pretend stuff.) In deference to Peter, kids consume both with equal gusto—and wash it down with this real green punch!

Crocodile Tears Punch

This recipe couldn't be easier, and can be made in a surprising variety of ways. I have successfully used other sodas, such as peach/ citrus Fresca mixed with Bacardi frozen margarita mix. However, it is not as wonderfully green—a problem solved with the addition of a few drops of green and yellow food coloring.

If you have a nice "tick-tock" clock, you could have it ticking away somewhere near the punch.

2 liters ginger ale
6 Lime Whole Fruit Bars
   (Edy's Fat-Free)
3 Key limes cut in half
1 kiwi fruit, peeled and sliced

Pour the ginger ale into a large punch bowl and add the fruit bars. After a few minutes, cut the fruit bars from their wooden sticks; add limes and kiwi fruit and serve.
   Yield: about 18 cups.

Opposite: You wouldn't believe the amount of green candy you can find if you really look. Maps and nautical gear help to tell the story. This croc is a three-dimensional puzzle toy.

A Christmas Carol

Ebenezer Scrooge hated Christmas. In fact, he hated nearly everything, for one reason or another. He was rich, secretive, and ruthless, and lived as a shriveled-up, miserly bachelor. One Christmas Eve, Scrooge's good-natured nephew Fred resolved to pester him a bit. He showed up at Scrooge's office to invite him over for Christmas dinner.

"Bah!—Humbug!" said Scrooge. "You keep Christmas in your way, and I'll keep it in mine."

"But you don't keep it."

"Let me leave it alone, then—much good has it ever done you!"

"Uncle, though it has never put a scrap of gold or silver in my pocket, I believe that it has done me good, and will do me good; and I say, God bless it!"

From his room in back, Scrooge's long-suffering clerk, Bob Cratchit, overheard the exchange and involuntarily applauded. As Scrooge let Fred out, two gentlemen came in asking for a donation for the poor. Scrooge dismissed them, opining that leaving the poor to their fate would effectively decrease the surplus population.

By the evening, Scrooge was fighting off a cold as he walked home to his dismal apartment. He was unnerved to find that his door-knocker had become the face of his deceased business partner, Jacob Marley. He went to his room and sat down. He saw an old bell in the room begin to swing slowly. The bell started to ring, and so did all the bells in the house.

*Scrooge's chair (right), next to the Ghost of Christmas Past.
Opposite: Has Marley's face mysteriously appeared on that easel?*

From the room below, he heard a clanking, dragging noise. The sound grew louder, coming up the stairs and into his room until it stood before him. It was the ghost of Jacob Marley! It dragged a heavy chain weighed down with cash boxes, deeds, and other tools of his earthly trade.

"Oh, woe is me!" cried the ghost. "I wear the chain I forged in life!"

Marley's shade explained that he was doomed to wander the world in penance for all the good he had failed to do on earth. He warned that Scrooge would share his fate unless he received visits from three more spirits on the next three nights. Then he departed.

Scrooge woke at midnight the following night. He was greeted by an elf who glowed and flickered like a candle flame. This "Ghost of Christmas Past" took Scrooge to scenes from his youth.

They saw a Christmas when schoolboy Scrooge stayed alone in a shabby room at his schoolmaster's, reading fairy tales. All the other boys had gone home to their families. The grown-up Scrooge wept. Then they saw him at a later Christmas, again alone at school. His little sister Fan burst in joyfully to tell him that his father was letting him come home. He recalled how much he'd loved her, and that she'd had a child before she died: his nephew Fred.

Then Scrooge saw the warehouse of his former employer, Fezziwig, during a dance for the employees on Christmas Eve. Scrooge noted that Fezziwig's spirit had the power to lighten people's burdens and make them happy. The party cost little, but for its effect, it might have cost a fortune.

He watched his fiancée break off their engagement because a fearful, restless avarice had taken hold of his heart and shut her out. The spirit then showed her happily married to another man, with a number of children. Scrooge's eyes grew dim when he realized that this exuberant family might have been his. He grabbed the glowing spirit's candle-snuffer hat and pushed it down, trying to put out the light, which still streamed onto the ground. He staggered to bed and fell asleep.

Scrooge awoke to find that it was the next night, and the clock had just struck one. A strange light came from the next room, which was hung with evergreen boughs and berries. A huge banquet was spread, and a giant in a green robe was sitting in the middle of it on a throne made of food.

The spirit introduced himself as the "Ghost of Christmas Present." He took Scrooge through the streets of London, where church bells rang and lush produce tempted passers-by. They arrived at Bob Cratchit's house, where the Cratchits savored their modest Christmas dinner with joy. Scrooge noticed that one of the boys, called Tiny Tim, was frail and thin, and moved about with a crutch.

"Spirit," said Scrooge with an interest he had never felt before, "tell me if Tiny Tim will live."

The ghost said that Tim would not survive another year, unless the future were changed. The shade added that Tim's death would effectively "decrease the surplus population." Scrooge was shocked to hear the crudeness of his own words quoted back to him.

They moved on to see Christmas being celebrated by miners; then to sea, where lighthouse keepers and sailors sang; and to hospitals, jails, and almshouses. At each place, the spirit left his blessing. They came to Fred's house, where he and his pretty wife were hosting a Christmas party with merriment and games. Scrooge longed to take part. At last, Fred announced:

"Here is a glass of mulled wine; and I say, 'Uncle Scrooge!' A Merry Christmas and a Happy New Year to the old man, wherever he is." The company joined in, and Scrooge was filled with joy.

Exactly at midnight, the ghost disappeared. As the reverberations of the last stroke died away, Scrooge saw a cloaked and hooded phantom coming toward him like a mist along the ground.

"The Ghost of Christmas Yet To Come" had no shape and did not speak, and took Scrooge to overhear some casual conversations about a recently deceased and unlamented man. In a filthy room, a "fence" named Joe dickered with some old women and the undertaker over payment for the shirt, bed-curtains, and other items they'd plundered from the dead man. The scene changed to the Cratchit household. Christmas decorations were hung, but the unusually quiet family was making burial preparations for their beloved Tiny Tim.

Finally, Scrooge was taken to a graveyard where the ghost pointed to the name on a tombstone: EBENEZER SCROOGE. He broke down and wept at the spirit's feet, begging for the chance to alter this bleak future. The ghost slowly shrank, dissolving into a bedpost—Scrooge's own bedpost!

Scrooge awoke to discover that his bed-curtains were still in place, and he was alive! He laughed. For a man who had been out of practice for so many years, it was an excellent laugh. Scrooge ran to the window and asked a boy in the street below what day it was. It was Christmas Day. He paid the boy to fetch the biggest turkey in the poulterer's window and have it sent to the Cratchit house.

He went to church, patted children on the head, and wished people a hearty "Merry Christmas!" He never dreamed that a simple walk, or that anything at all, could yield so much happiness. Still giddy, he made his way to Fred's house for Christmas dinner.

The next morning, Scrooge raised Cratchit's salary. He became a second father to Tiny Tim, who did not die after all. And ever after, it was said of Scrooge:

He became as good a friend, as good a master, and as good a man, as the good old city knew. And he knew how to keep Christmas well.

Scrooge and the Christmas Cure

To be, or not to be... a Scrooge.

That question perennially haunts the human race. On the one hand are the Christmas enthusiasts like Scrooge's nephew Fred, who love the celebration with all its grandeur, rollicking excesses, and silliness. Arrayed against them are those who find the whole business annoying. To quote Scrooge:

"Every idiot who goes about with 'Merry Christmas' on his lips should be boiled with his own pudding, and buried with a stake of holly through his heart."

Since happiness and misery both love company, the question is: Which side are you on?

Throughout history, scorn has been endured, fines have been levied, and punishments have been served for celebrating Christmas. Foods traditionally associated with the holiday (such as mince pie) were banned from Puritan England. Soldiers were ordered to patrol the streets of London and confiscate any food being cooked for a Christmas dinner. In our own times, a school administration tried to stop kids from wearing red and green. Another school canceled a stage performance at the last minute, saying the subject matter was too religious. It was a dramatization of *A Christmas Carol*.

But if you think the Christmas wars are merely a religious conflict, think again. Government institutions today claim the holiday is too Christian to allow in the public square. Just as many church leaders denounce the eating and gift-giving as scandalously secular. People from both sides say the holiday is artificial, invented to displace a Roman sun festival on that day. Yet there had been no sun festival in early winter until Emperor Aurelian created Saturnalia on December 25, 274. Did he have a problem with Christmas too?

"Thou wilt incline the hearts of the citizens . . . to entertain a brotherly affection and love for one another."

—George Washington, inaugural prayer

I think it's Christmas itself, as a physical celebration, that is the real issue. Nine out of ten Scrooges of all faiths, ancient and modern, gripe most vocally about all the money spent on gifts, the overeating of rich food, and the open, intimate feeling that inspires people to wish happiness to complete strangers.

Charles Dickens had a revolutionary insight that would only become understood 75 years later with the growth of psychoanalysis. He showed that Scrooge's hostility to his fellow man is what is now called an "attachment disorder" that originated in his childhood, when he was virtually abandoned by his family. Scrooge has come to rely on himself alone to survive. Any hint of connection to other human beings, as either a dependent or a benefactor, is abominable and frightening to him, and he wants to blot it out.

Scrooge's cynicism is a mask. He hates Christmas because, more than any other time of year, it reminds him that he is weak. He hates seeing people wish each other good cheer and thereby declare their dependence on one another. He lacks a key ingredient of sanity: confidence in the existence of genuine good will.

The ghost takes Scrooge on a journey to his youth, where he is able to observe himself as a child. The floodgate of his emotions opens up, and sadness and joy come pouring back into his soul. In this passive state, he sees things as they truly are. With his emotions unlocked from their prison, he is able to recognize the beauty of human existence for the first time, and to experience gratitude, compassion, happiness, and love.

Dickens, who had a childhood similar to Scrooge's, recognized that Christmas sets us free. He implies that, by trying to keep what little we have, we lose even that; but in giving ourselves away, we gain everything.

Left: The doorway at the eastern entrance to Lyndhurst, hung with a garland of pears. On either side of the door are topiaries made of blown-glass ornaments glued around foam ball and cone forms.

Opposite: A bust of George Washington in Lyndhurst's foyer is set off by a garland decorated with red poinsettia brachts. To secure each bracht on the garland, its stem is bent into a hook, pushed into the garland, and then pulled back so it catches on a branch.

Overleaf: The busts of Washington (left) and the Marquis de Lafayette were installed by the house's first owner, William Paulding. As Mayor of New York, Paulding welcomed Lafayette on his return to America.

Scrooge's tree, visible in the reception room at the end of the hall, is decorated with traditional "Christmas crackers." (One with gold-foil ends is visible in close-up on page 118.) These party favors, which make a gratifying gunpowder "bang!" when pulled apart, were invented in England around the time Dickens was writing "A Christmas Carol."

The Stuffing of Dreams

This stuffing is no mere ornament to the meat. By itself, it could fatten up Tiny Tim. Dream or no dream, it could have made Scrooge love his fellow man—or at least, the cook.

The Stuffing of Dreams

There's nothing wrong with "interesting" stuffing—raisin-chutney-balsamic-whatever. But it's Christmas! When you serve this stuffing, you actually make people happy, and they don't stop eating until the platter is empty.

1 long loaf ordinary sliced white bread
1/2 roll (6 ounces) frozen pork
    sausage (I prefer Jones All-Natural)
3 sticks celery with leaves, chopped
1 medium yellow onion, chopped
Salt and pepper to taste
2–3 parsley stalks, minced
3–5 fresh sage leaves, minced
1/2 can chicken broth (8 ounces),
    or as needed

Ahead of time, cut bread into 5/8-inch cubes and spread onto a cookie sheet. Dry in a 250-degree oven. Check at 10-minute intervals, stirring occasionally so bread doesn't toast.

Thoroughly cook sausage in a large frying pan. Add celery and onion; cook about five more minutes. Toss with bread cubes in a large bowl, adding salt, pepper, parsley, and sage.

If you're stuffing a turkey, stuff the bird first. Then take the remaining stuffing and put into one (large) or two (small) baking pans. Add a small amount of chicken broth to the stuffing in the pans to keep it from drying out.

Cook turkey as directed for its weight; cover pans with foil and cook for 30 minutes at 325 degrees.

Yield: 8 cups.

Above: What you smell when you walk into a bustling house where a turkey is cooking is actually the stuffing. Sausage, celery, and sage ensure that the Ghost of Christmas Present will give his blessing.

The Snow Queen

A wicked hobgoblin made a mirror that had the power of making everything good or beautiful that was reflected in it shrink to almost nothing. Everything worthless and bad seen in this mirror increased in size. The most lovely landscapes appeared like boiled spinach, and people became hideous and looked as if they stood on their heads and had no bodies.

Pretty soon, the demon had amused himself silly by looking at the whole world in this way. He kept a school of philosophy, and all who went there declared that it was now possible to see the world and mankind as they really are.

One day a couple of demons got hold of the hobgoblin's mirror and tried to fly it to heaven to look at the angels. But the mirror grew slippery and crashed to the ground, shattering into a million sharp pieces, each of which had the same ability to distort as the original glass. This is the story of what happened with one of them.

Two poor young children in the city loved to play together—a boy named Kay and a girl named Gerda. They lived in neighboring rooftop apartments, between which their families had planted window boxes of roses. The roses were beautiful in the summer.

Gerda taught Kay a little hymn about roses that went, *"Roses bloom and cease to be; But we shall the Christ-child see."*

Above and previous pages: The Snow Queen's sleigh is an antique pram with runners. It sits on a "pond" of mirror tiles.

Often Kay's grandmother told them stories. One evening when she told them about the Snow Queen, Kay impatiently declared that, should he ever meet her, he would melt her on the stove. A few days later, Kay was watching at the window when a large snowflake alighted on the edge of one of the flower boxes and grew larger until it became a woman in garments of snowflakes. The Snow Queen nodded and waved to him; she was beautiful and quite perfect, but there was neither peace nor rest in her eyes.

Soon it was summer, and Kay was with Gerda by the roses when he felt something go into his heart and his eye. They were splinters of the goblin's mirror; they distorted his vision and quickly turned his heart to a lump of ice.

"Why do you cry?" Kay suddenly asked Gerda. "It makes you look ugly." He noticed that one of the roses on the bush was worm-eaten, and another crooked. He kicked the window boxes and pulled off the two roses. After that, began to spend his time mimicking and ridiculing other people. (Some adults thought he was quite clever.)

Looking at snowflakes under a magnifier fascinated him. "Look in this glass, Gerda," said he. "There is not a single fault in it: Snow-flakes are quite perfect till they begin to melt."

The Snow Queen arrived one winter day, circling her sleigh around the square, where the boys would hitch their sleds to the back of country people's carts to get a ride. Kay hitched to her sleigh, and it began to move. Faster and faster it went, and he could not unhitch his sled from it.

Kay was frightened and tried saying his prayers—but he could remember nothing but the multiplication table. Farther and farther they went, to the Snow Queen's palace in the cold, dark north.

Kay was gone, and no one knew where. Little Gerda wept bitterly for him, believing he was dead. But the sun and the birds told her they didn't believe it. Gerda set off to look for him.

Down the river, she met a sorceress who tried to make her forget Kay and stay with her. But the roses growing in the garden told her Kay was still alive—they had not seen him under the ground. Gerda escaped and traveled north, helped by a strange robber-girl who gave her a reindeer to ride.

Finally, Gerda and the reindeer arrived at the hut of a conjurer called the Finland Woman. The reindeer begged the woman to give Gerda the strength of twelve men, to overcome the Snow Queen's power. But the woman replied, "She cannot receive any power from me greater than that she now has, which consists in her own purity and innocence of heart."

The little girl had fogotten her mittens and boots at the Finland Woman's hut, and made the last part of her journey barefoot and alone in the bitter cold. The snowflakes around her grew bigger, came to life, and started to attack her. As she prayed aloud, the steam from her breath formed a legion of angels, who thrust their spears into the snowflakes and shattered them.

At last she reached the Snow Queen's palace. The walls were made of drifted snow, with more than a hundred rooms, lighted by the *Aurora Borealis*. They were huge and empty, with no toys—not even a little ball to play with or a tea-table to sit at.

Gerda found Kay sitting in the middle of a vast, empty hall on a frozen lake called the "Mirror of Reason." He was blue with cold, playing at the game of reason with identical puzzle pieces of ice. The Snow Queen was away—gone to the warmer countries to bring snow to the tops of the volcanoes and a change of season to help the lemons and grapes grow.

Oblivious to the cold, Kay dragged pieces of ice to and fro, making different words and figures with them. But there was one word that he could not spell, much as he wanted to. The Snow Queen had promised that he would be his own master and have the whole world and a new pair of skates if he could spell it. That word was ETERNITY.

Gerda ran to him and threw her arms around him. But he sat there stiff and cold. She began to weep, and as her hot little tears fell on him they thawed his frozen heart and washed away the glass sliver.

She sang, *"Roses bloom and cease to be; But we shall the Christ-child see."*

Kay recognized her at last and burst into tears, and the splinter of glass swam out of his eye.

He clung to her and said joyfully, "Gerda, dear little Gerda, where have you been all this time, and where have I been?" She laughed and wept for joy. The puzzle-pieces danced about, and then formed themselves into letters that spelled "ETERNITY."

Kay and Gerda left the palace. After a long journey, they arrived back home as the church bells were pealing merrily. When they reached Kay's grandmother's door, they realized that they were now grown, and had become man and woman.

Hand in hand, they sat in the bright sunshine by the grandmother. She was in her chair, reading aloud: "Except ye become as little children . . ." They were grown up, yet children at heart. And it was summer—warm, beautiful summer.

The Aurora Borealis over Lyndhurst. (Photo by Rob Yasinsac)

Ice Palace

It may be that Gerda's tears have thawed more than Kay's heart, because the Snow Queen seems to have softened up a bit. She's installed a Christmas tree in her formerly bleak bedroom. On the advice of a good decorator, she has begun to pay more attention to proportion, balance, and the beauty of irregularity. This has helped her achieve a more welcoming atmosphere without sacrificing her personal style. It looks as if she might even be expecting some (non-captive) visitors!

While she still prefers an all-white color scheme, the Snow Queen now uses lights to illuminate the snow crystals hanging on the branches of her Christmas tree, dispelling some of the dismal darkness. The ornaments are a fantasy of icicles, snowflakes, and glass figurines. Faux crystal-tipped branches are mixed in with the regular branches. Finally, handfuls of tinsel are stuffed inside the boughs toward the trunk to reflect the lights and increase the shimmer.

Instead of that endless, boring lake in the middle of her great hall, she now has a small pond made of 12x12-inch mirror tiles placed together on the floor. Around the edge is a bank of faux snow, which softens the rectangular perimeters.

Right: The Snow Queen's tree in the South Bedroom. Previous pages, left: A detail of the tree; right: Her all-white tree in the Northeast Bedroom.

Sleigh Ride

You know you're in for a wild ride at the beginning of "The Snow Queen." It starts with a subplot about a bunch of demons playing with a mirror that makes good seem evil, and evil good. The author whose mighty pen produced the biting satire, "The Emperor's New Suit," is preparing to demolish another group of self-important intellectuals, and he is in no mood to take prisoners. Grab some popcorn and a good seat.

Hans Christian Andersen soon starts dropping hints about who he's after: He tells us that the demons have a school of philosophy, where they become so full of their own ideas that they try their tricks on heaven. But it doesn't work, and their mischief falls back to earth, where it does a lot of damage.

Then he drops another hint: Kay becomes disgusted with human imperfection, represented by the roses, which grow crookedly, wilt, and get attacked by worms. He is fascinated by perfection, represented by the snowflakes—which he says are quite perfect "until they begin to melt." And so the Snow Queen takes him to a place where there are no imperfect humans and no roses, where he can explore the frozen wasteland of his own ideas.

The *dénouement* is when Andersen shows us Kay, sitting frozen on the "Mirror of Reason," trying to shape tiny, identical puzzle pieces into different designs and words.

Even the Snow Queen points out to Kay that he will have neither mastery over himself nor freedom unless he can spell one single word: ETERNITY.

Le Coeur a ses raisons que la Raison ne connait point.

(The heart has its reasons,
of which reason knows nothing.)

—Blaise Pascal

And of course he can't, since he doesn't understand the bigger perfection hidden in human imperfection.

Enter Gerda, who represents childlike simplicity and love. The tears she weeps for Kay make even the ice pieces dance, forming the word ETERNITY by themselves.

When Andersen wrote "The Snow Queen" in 1844, the French Revolution and ensuing reign of terror were recent history. In the name of the "Goddess of Reason," the revolutionaries killed their imperfect king and substituted a series of murderous dictatorships. They tried to improve the world by destroying human institutions and replacing them with their own inventions. Like Kay, they were fascinated with perfection.

The revolutionaries divided time into perfect units of ten: Ten minutes per hour, ten hours per day, ten days per week. People and animals balked at working nine days without a break, and the plan was kept alive only by neighborhood informers. The autocrats ordered the people to use new units of weight and measure such as the kilogram—but there were riots in the streets of Paris because there was no bread to weigh.

The empire of Reason crumbled because it could not spell "reality," never mind "eternity."

That age gave way to the Romantic Era. There was a new recognition that imagination is a path to truth, and that man's imperfection is also his glory. Romantic architecture seeks to unite buildings with the natural landscape. Its literature draws on folk culture, which inspired Andersen, the Grimms, and others to enthrall millions with an art form known as the fairy tale.

Northern Delights

The Snow Queen was not noted for her warm hospitality
and got few visitors. But in a pinch she could whip up one or two
impressive desserts using fresh local ingredients—such as ice.

Snow Cream

*Like Kay's ride behind the Snow Queen's
sleigh, once you start eating Snow Cream, it's
hard to stop. At first, it seems like old-fashioned
ice cream; but if you eat it too fast, your head
will get so numb you could forget your prayers
and possibly your name. Enjoy it safely!*

2 cups ice cubes (about seven square cubes)
1 cup heavy cream
1/4 teaspoon vanilla
1/4 cup real maple syrup
1/4 teaspoon salt

Crush the ice in a blender; add the
cream and continue blending until the mix
is like slush. Add vanilla, syrup, and salt; blend
again until it is like melted ice cream. Drink it
like a shake or pour it into a bowl and freeze
it a while to make it more like a "slushy."
Yield: 2–4 servings.

Aurora Borealis

*This is basically Snow Cream, with berries
instead of ice. The same warnings apply!*

2 cups frozen mixed berries—or
  21/2–3 cups frozen strawberries
1 cup heavy cream
1/2 cup real maple syrup
Pinch of salt

Crush the berries together with
the cream in a blender; add the syrup
and salt and blend until smooth.
Yield: 2–4 servings.

*Foreground: Snow Cream served in a craquelle goblet—sometimes called "ice glass" because of
its finely crackled surface. Background: Strawberry and mixed-berry Aurora Borealis.*

The Nutcracker Ballet

In the middle of a Christmas Eve Party at the von Stahlbaum house, the door suddenly swings open and a mysterious figure enters. The assembled company's shock turns to delight as they realize that it is Herr Drosselmeyer, young Clara von Stahlbaum's beloved godfather. Clara is possibly even more delighted when he introduces his handsome young nephew.

Drosselmeyer is a clock and toy maker, and apparently something of a magician. He winds the von Stahlbaum's large clock and amuses the children with wonderful mechanical toys (played onstage by dancers) that seem to come to life.

Finally, he pulls out a nutcracker that looks like a prince and starts using it to shell nuts for the children. Everyone wants the nutcracker, but he gives it to Clara. So as not to leave anyone out, he gives china dolls to the other girls and toy swords to the boys. A lot of rambunctious play ensues, during which Clara's younger brother Fritz breaks the nutcracker.

A detail of the Nutcracker's tree. Previous pages, left: The tree in the East Bedroom; Right: face of a tall case clock by Tiffany & Company presented to Jay Gould as a housewarming gift.

Clara is traumatized, and Herr Drosselmeyer bandages the nutcracker with his handkerchief. After the guests have left and the children are in bed, Clara tiptoes back to the parlor to check on her nutcracker. She falls asleep near the Christmas tree, with the nutcracker close by her.

As the clock strikes midnight, the house takes on a whole new life: The Christmas tree becomes huge, the room turns into a forest, and an army of nasty, human-sized rats and mice show up to steal the food. Clara is terrified—but her Nutcracker has also grown to life size. With his army of toy soldiers he battles the rodents to defend her. Just as it seems that the King of the Rats is about to overcome the Nutcracker and his men, Clara sneaks up behind and strikes the King with her slipper. It distracts him long enough for the Nutcracker to deal him a fatal blow. But alas, the Nutcracker is wounded also, and falls to the ground.

Then Clara's grief turns to amazement. Her Nutcracker stirs, turns into a real young Prince (who looks a lot like Drosselmeyer's nephew), and takes her hand. In some versions of the ballet, he presents the defeated Rat King's sword to Drosselmeyer, who turns it into a crown, which the prince places on Clara's head.

The Prince helps Clara into a sleigh and they begin a ride through a snowy, moonlit forest. As they watch, the snowflakes grow and turn into dancing fairies.

In the second act, Clara and the Prince arrive in the Kingdom of Sweets at the palace of the Sugar Plum Fairy, who is delighted when they tell her about the Rat King's defeat. She gives them seats of honor in her court, and prepares for them a mystical feast resembling a wedding banquet. They are entertained by exotic gifts, which come dancing to life:

Arabian coffee is represented by a group of sultry harem girls whose billowing veils mimic clouds of steam rising from the cup. Ginger is a jovial matron with dozens of gingerbread children capering around the stage causing mischief. Other dances portray angels, Chinese tea, marzipan, Spanish chocolate, swirling flowers, and leaping Cossacks.

Finally, there is a breathtaking *pas de deux* between the Sugar Plum Fairy and her consort, the Cavalier. The pageant finishes, Clara and the Prince bid farewell to their hostess, and the magic sleigh returns to take them home.

Clara awakes to find herself in the parlor of her house. It is Christmas morning, and she is still holding her nutcracker.

Poetry of the Air

All stands in readiness for a Christmas Eve party at Clara von Stahlbaum's house—where magical things are about to happen.

On with the dance!
let joy be unconfined;

No sleep till morn,
when youth
and pleasure meet

To chase
the glowing hours
with flying feet.

—Lord Byron

Above left: The Nutcracker's tree in Lyndhurst's dining room. Above right: A fruit compote; beyond, antiques from Lyndhurst's collection. Left: A sconce in the dining room. The wall behind it is painted to look like tooled and gilded leather. Overleaf: Detail of the compote. The first layer of faux sugared fruit is hot-glued onto a circle of corrugated cardboard cut to fit inside the bowl. Each additional layer is glued onto the last, with leaves and smaller fruits filling the gaps. See diagrams and instructions, page 152.

Clara's Tiara

Some of the most moving scenes in *The Nutcracker* reflect the theology of the Russian Orthodox Church. In the 1977 version choreographed and performed by Mikhail Baryshnikov (available as a PBS Video), the Nutcracker assumes a crucified position when he falls after his battle with the Rat King. Russian spirituality emphasizes the husband's duty of self-sacrifice.

Other elements echo the Orthodox marriage rite, which contains, like the ballet, a candlelight procession to guide the couple in their new life together. It ends with a crowning ceremony: Crowns, a reward for victory over evil, are placed on the heads of the husband and wife. From this moment they are recognized as king and queen of a new household. Sweet treats served at the banquet (like the exotic gifts in the ballet) symbolize the sweetness of married life.

This Russian wedding coronation rite goes back well over a thousand years, and actually predates an official Christian rite of marriage. It may have its roots in even more ancient Jewish tradition. The Hebrew word for bride *(kallah)* comes from the word for crown *(kelil)*, indicating wholeness, perfection, and culmination.

By crowning Clara, the Prince declares that each of them makes the other, for the first time, complete.

140

Reclaiming Eden

Why is this tale so popular that it is performed more than any other ballet? At the premiere of the music, *The Nutcracker Suite,* in the spring of 1892, the audience went wild, demanding immediate encores for six of the movements.

The ballet had its premiere in St. Petersburg later that year on December 17th. Czar Alexander III, a patron of the composer, Pyotr Ilyich Tchaikovsky, loved the performance. Connoisseurs of ballet took seats in the upper tier of the theater so they could see the swirling patterns made by the sixty dancers performing the Waltz of the Snowflakes.

But the critics hated it.
From a review of that first performance: "For dancers there is rather little in it, for art, absolutely nothing, and for the artistic fate of our ballet, one more step downward."

Modern authorities like the ballet no better. Dance critic Richard Buckle famously began a review, "Well, we are all one *Nutcracker* nearer death."

Another writer complains that it has "a distinctly thin plot and characters it is difficult to care much about," and lacks interest for an adult audience.

I was an adult myself before I went to my first *Nutcracker,* but I've now been to four, and don't intend to stop soon. I think a fair number of us adults use "taking the kids" as a handy excuse to see it ourselves. Here is a sampling of people I saw at a recent amateur performance held in a small city nearby:

Little and big girls come dressed in ringlets, ribbons, and velvet. A little girl arrives with her daddy in a coffee-cup-and-newspaper-strewn pickup. During intermission, as he pauses for a cigarette in the vestibule, she runs up to give him a bear-hug. They are both beaming.

When Clara is crowned, an elderly gentleman in the back sniffs into his handkerchief; periodically, I notice other people choking back tears. As the stage erupts into color during the "Waltz of the Flowers," a two-year-old boy roars "HA! HA!" in delight.

The Nutcracker stands ready to battle the Rat King. Overleaf, Christmas heroes: Nutcrackers, toy soldiers, and Santas.

The entire audience cheers as a teenage boy from the local public high school leads a precise and athletic *trepak*—the traditional Cossack men's dance.

At every performance I have seen, several little girls in the audience succumb to the urge to bolt from their seats and start twirling and dancing in the aisles.

What do all these people intuitively understand that critics so utterly miss?

The Nutcracker is a simple tale. Is it shallow? No. Based on Alexandre Dumas's retelling of E.T.A. Hoffmann's story, "The Nutcracker and the King of Mice," it's about Clara, an archetypal young girl whose magical dream shows her how she will become a woman. Her brother Fritz represents the impulsiveness of childhood. Drosselmeyer is a godfather in every sense: a spiritual mentor and symbol of Father Time, with a touch of God the Father. He is a mysterious, doting presence who creates, guides, and assists, but does not compel.

Drosselmeyer's nephew is young manhood—noble and idealistic, with a slight over-estimation of his own powers. The Rat King (Hoffmann's Mouse King) clearly stands for evil: devouring, menacing, and destructive. In Hoffmann, he has seven heads like the beast of the Apocalypse.

The Rat King is more powerful than either Clara or her Prince individually, but when they are united, he is defeated. As if to drive the marriage symbolism home, the Sugar Plum Fairy's dance with her Cavalier offers a transparent hint that this Adam-and-Eve thing might not have been such a bad idea after all.

We are accustomed to the jaded assumption that growing up means a loss of innocence. The genius of *The Nutcracker* is its vision of Eden revisited, where the gifts of adulthood are enhanced by the nobility and innocence of youth. It affirms that growing up is not meant to be a betrayal of childhood, but its fulfillment.

Coffee & Sugar Plums

Listening to Tchaikovsky's "Arabian Dance" gives a hint
of the exotic, other-worldly taste of this traditionally brewed coffee.

Arabian Coffee

*Recommended beans: Ethiopian Longberry
Harrar or Yergacheffe; Eight O'Clock Coffee's
regular or Bokar Blends (from Central and
South America) also work. Avoid dark roasts.*

    23/4 cups water
    21/2 scoops coffee beans (5 tablespoons)
    4 teaspoons sugar
    1/4 teaspoon vanilla extract
    1/4 teaspoon allspice
    1/4 teaspoon cardamom
    1/4 teaspoon cinnamon
    1/4 teaspoon ground cloves
    1/4 teaspoon ground ginger
    1/4 teaspoon anise (whole)

Grind beans "Turkish" style—a virtual
powder. Add all ingredients (except anise)
to water in a saucepan and heat until frothy.
Remove from heat, stir in anise. Let settle
1 minute and serve. Pour from the top to
keep grounds in the saucepan.
    Yield: 2–3 cups.

Sugar Plums

*There are nearly as many recipes for sugar
plums as there are Sugar Plum fairies. Flavor
is best if you make sugar plums a few days
ahead and store covered in the refrigerator.*

    3/4 cup pecans
    1/4 cup dried apricots
    1/4 cup dates
    1/4 cup dried figs
    1/4 cup dried cranberries

    2 tablespoons honey
    2 tablespoons unsweetened cocoa powder
    2 teaspoons almond extract
    1 teaspoon Cointreau or other orange liqueur
    1/4 teaspoon allspice
    1/4 teaspoon freshly ground nutmeg
    1/2 teaspoon cinnamon
    1/2 cup granulated or colored sugar for coating

In a blender, combine the pecans and
dried fruit until bits are not much bigger
than peppercorns, then transfer to a bowl.
    In a separate bowl, mix the honey
with the cocoa powder, almond extract,
liqueur, and spices. Add to the fruit mixture, and blend thoroughly by hand.
    Form and roll into balls about 7/8 of an inch
in diameter; roll in granulated sugar to coat.
    Yield: about 30 sugar plums.

*Visions of sugar plums: Taste one, and you'll know why Clara dreamed of them. Opposite: Arabian coffee, served in
royal blue- and gold-banded lustreware, circa 1890. The teapot is a modern Russian import, bearing the firebird motif.*

Notes from an Enchanted Castle
The Story of Lyndhurst

To begin with, Lyndhurst is not a castle.
I know what you're thinking: It *looks* like a castle.
But it's not fortified to repel attackers. It has never
been a seat of government—no kings or princes live
there, except fairy-tale ones. And the place doesn't even
have a proper moat, unless you count the Hudson River
churning majestically in the distance.

Properly speaking, Lyndhurst, in Tarrytown, N.Y.,
is a "Gothic Revival Mansion." It's a large house built
in the style of a medieval castle. The exterior is only a
stone facade designed to look like huge stone blocks.
The "marble" hallways are not marble, but artfully
painted plaster and wood. The dining room walls, which
look like tooled leather, are covered only with paint
and gilding. The house is a fantasy, meant to pique the
imagination and make the spirit soar. It is not mere
protection from the elements; it is meant to be enjoyed.
In short, it is the perfect home for fairy tales.

General William Paulding (1770–1854) finished
the building of the house in 1842. At that time, New
York City had just begun to boom as a world port, and
portions of Westchester County's farms were being sold
to create country estates. Paulding had been a Congress-
man and a mayor of New York City, and was a veteran
of the War of 1812. His neighbor to the south was
world-famous author Washington Irving.

Why did Gen. Paulding build a castle? First of all,
on a rugged hill overlooking the River, that's what the
land demanded, according to the architectural theories
of the early nineteenth century. Earlier, at the time of
the Founders and in the aftermath of the American
Revolution, the fashions demanded spare, symmetri-
cal, neoclassical buildings based on Greek and Roman
structures. The new architecture, Romantic, was more
fun. The Romantics held that a great house's duty is to
reflect both nature and the personality of the family that
lives there—its imagination and its emotions. To capture all that in a house, architects borrowed exotic styles
and features from all over the world: Greek, Egyptian,
Oriental, Gothic, Romanesque, Swiss, and more.

The architect for Knoll, as the house was
first called, was Alexander Jackson Davis (1803–1892),
the foremost architect of his day, who supervised the
construction himself. He designed not only the house
exterior, but some of the fixtures and furniture, so that
they would be part of the masterpiece.

Gen. Paulding died in 1854. Ten years later, the
house was sold to inventor and merchant George Merritt, who had four children. Apparently he liked what
he had and wanted more of it, because he chose as his
architect . . . Alexander Jackson Davis. Merritt made
the "castle" bigger and higher, adding ornate plaster

Amaryllis bulbs bloom in the medieval-inspired window on the staircase that leads to the upper floors.

decorations on the ceilings, wall-to-wall carpets, and crystal chandeliers. He called the expanded mansion Lyndenhurst.

Merritt died in 1873. Wall Street financier Jay Gould and his family began renting the house in 1878 and bought it in 1880 for $255,000, shortening its name to Lyndhurst. He and his wife, Helen, and their six children spent summers and holidays there—including Christmas. The furnishings now on display at Lyndhurst are mostly those of the Merritts and the Goulds.

Though he had vast national influence—and a reputation for ruthlessness in the business world—Jay Gould was a private man with a low-key home life. He kept on the same gardener from the Merritt years; Gould himself planted trees with his children.

For a big house, Lyndhurst is not pretentious; it's almost intimate. The rooms aren't large—but their high ceilings create a feeling of grandeur. Photographs show that the rooms were not merely for display but were thoroughly lived in. In a photograph of one of the boys' bedrooms, there are books piled everywhere, ties hanging on several light fixtures, and a pennant over the bed.

Helen Gould, Jay's philanthropist daughter, also had a desk covered with books, and kept a medieval madonna on the wall beside her bed. Her room is believed to have been her father's before her; it seems almost cramped. The Goulds had no soaring, 22-karat gilt reception room (unlike the Vanderbilts), and no museum (unlike the Rockefellers). There is a modest art collection and a big greenhouse—but no ballroom. Helen opened the greenhouse to the public and sponsored a sewing school for local girls in the estate's pavilions. After she died in 1938, Lyndhurst was sold to her youngest sister, Anna, the Duchess of Talleyrand-Perigord (France). At her death in 1961, Anna left it to its current owner, the National Trust for Historic Preservation.

As you get to know Lyndhurst, awe-inspiring though it is, you begin to see that the rich are bound by the laws of gravity, nature, and leaky roofs like the rest of us. What the house's creators had was a big dose of confidence: confidence to have fun with an idea and bring it to life. The magical thing about Lyndhurst is not its materials, which are ordinary, but what it looks like.

The impressive arched doorways look like stone. In fact, they are bigger versions of the wood moldings in your house and mine—painted in a color you might call "fairy-tale castle stone gray." And with a ladder, a stencil, and some gold paint, you, too, can have stars on your bedroom ceiling like those in the Star Bedroom. Those with money can pay others to dream their dreams for them, executed in plaster and paint. Those with imagination can achieve similar glories—if they dare.

Lyndhurst today is considered one of the finest surviving examples of nineteenth-century architecture in America. But greatness often is too bold to be recognized in its own time. Philip Hone, another former New York mayor, was a political rival of Gen. Paulding's. He saw the house being built, with its "towers, turrets and trellises; archways, armories and airholes." He concluded that the house "will one of these days be designated as 'Paulding's folly.' "

That day has not arrived. I doubt it ever will.

The Quiet Man

Jay Gould, the third owner of Lyndhurst, was easily its richest—as a matter of fact, he was the eighth-richest American in history. Vanderbilt and Astor are above him on the list, and Bill Gates is still far below at number 31.

Born Jason Gould near upstate Roxbury, New York, in 1836, he studied mathematics and surveying, working in hardware and banking. Moving to New York, he ran a tanning business and became a stockbroker. He took over the failing Rutland & Washington railway, taught himself the railroad business, and turned the company profitable. Over the next several years, he earned the grudging respect of the big financial players.

Gould married Helen Day Miller in 1863. They had six children, and unlike flashier tycoons, Gould was utterly devoted to his wife and family to the end of his days.

In 1867, Gould was elected to the board of the Erie railway. At that time, big companies dueled like rival gangs. Although personally unassuming and deliberate, Gould was decisive in action, and much resented.

English bondholders charged in a lawsuit that Gould had sold them fraudulent stock in the Erie. In the same period, Gould and his partner James Fisk, aiming to increase traffic on the Erie, touched off a panic in 1869 when they tried to corner the gold market. Gould was forced out of the Erie in 1872, but it barely slowed him down. He gained control of the Union Pacific and Missouri Pacific railways, and by 1880 controlled one-ninth of the railway mileage in the United States. He

Jay Gould's portrait hangs above the fireplace in the room that was his home office. The bronze and marble clock set (called a "mantel garniture") was made in Philadelphia by Bailey, Banks and Biddle.

also ran the Western Union Telegraph Company, plus all New York's elevated trains.

The newspapers vilified and caricatured him. He endured regular threats, a beating, a bombing, and kidnap attempts against his family. One of his business rivals described Gould as "the worst man on earth since the beginning of the Christian era." But Gould's business tactics were typical at that time. Only his strategic sense was unique. He humiliated his competitors by what today is called "thinking outside the box."

The great Commodore Cornelius Vanderbilt, owner of the New York Central Railroad, was trying to destroy the Erie's business so he could force Gould to sell it to him. To capture the Erie's customers, Vanderbilt reduced the price of shipping a carload of cattle to New York from $125 to $1—an absurd price far below cost.

When Vanderbilt's agents came to him with reports of cars going empty on the Erie, he was overjoyed. He didn't realize that Gould and his partner James Fisk, rather than continuing a rate war against the better-financed Vanderbilt, had decided to use the New York's low rates to their advantage. They bought all available steers coming into Buffalo from the western U.S.—and instead of using their own railroad, sent them on the Commodore's trains. Selling the cattle in New York, they pocketed a huge profit, courtesy of Vanderbilt.

Gould, who kept an exhausting schedule all his life, contracted tuberculosis—but maintained his businesses and his gardening to the end. When he died in 1892, he left his entire fortune of $72 million to his family.

Making Magic
Create a Fairy Tale in Your Living Room

Do try this at home!

As the Snow Queen's room was being set up at Lyndhurst last year, a few stray bits of dried leaf ended up on the "snow banks" beside the mirror lake. Someone joked, "It adds a bit of realism."

Robert (Bob) Pesce, the exhibit's designer, shot back, "We don't want reality. We want fantasy!"

It's true. Looking into a room at Lyndhurst at Christmastime is like looking inside a Fabergé egg. Through the doorway, you are greeted by a scene so exotic and complete, it takes you to another world.

When he isn't doing Christmas displays, Bob designs displays for department stores and wholesale trade shows. He told me the three most important factors in professional displays are the **product**, the **place-**ment, and the **lighting**. Whether you're decorating the window of a showroom or a Christmas tree in your living room, the crucial things are the same: what to use, where to put it, and how to light it.

A decorating strategy based on the way Bob applied these ideas at Lyndhurst starts with the right tools (below). Then follow the steps to create your own display.

Bob's Tool Kit
Several hot glue guns and plenty of sticks
24-gauge green floral wire
Nylon fishing line (5-pound test)
Round-nose pliers with clippers (rosary pliers)
Scissors
A hammer and some nails
A staple gun and staples
Adhesive-backed Velcro strips
A good hand cream or salve
Extra ribbon
A notebook or sketchbook
A sturdy ladder or step-stool

THE 7 STEPS TO HIGHLY MAGICAL CHRISTMAS DISPLAYS

1) Make a map.

Six months or more ahead of time, Bob makes a quick diagram of a room he plans to decorate, locating the windows, door, and mantelpiece as seen from above. He sketches in the tree and balances it with garlands on other main features in the room.

In your sketch (use a tape measure for scale), place the tree so you see its full impact as you approach or enter the room—framed by the doorway (see illustration opposite). Also note the room's dominant colors.

2) Decide on a theme; pick colors carefully.

If you're building your display around a fairy tale, think about the colors associated with it—for instance, people think of greens for "Peter Pan" or white and silver for "The Snow Queen." On the other hand, a color palette can be inspired by almost anything beautiful: a peacock feather or a favorite magazine clipping.

Themes and colors for the Lyndhurst display are sometimes suggested by the rooms themselves. The starry-ceilinged Star Bedroom with its canopy bed was obviously a perfect dreamland for Sleeping Beauty.

Keep your eyes open for ornaments and supplies in colors related to your theme.

In addition to scouting for supplies, Bob spends some of his downtime during the summer making bows, compotes, and other small-scale decorations for the rooms. (For diagrams, see pages 154 and 157.)

3) Define the space.
I asked Bob: When he's decorating an area, how does he decide what should go where?

Without hesitation, he answered: "By how the space is used. You don't put a tree in the middle of a hallway—somebody will trip over it. But you might run a garland along the ceiling." Here are some ideas for how to set the scene:

Use the architecture. The tree in a room should be balanced by one or two other focal points that can be hung with garlands. Most frequently, these are windows and fireplace mantels, but other possible points include chandeliers, doorways, arches, tables, and mirrors.

Consider dramatic (temporary) room changes. Some of the most gratifying effects are created by adding a floor covering to concentrate the visitor's view on a certain "stage" area. One-foot square mirror tiles from a home-improvement warehouse created the Snow Queen's frozen lake. Artificial snow billows from behind the furniture in Snow-White's room. Alice's tree is sitting on a floor of 1-foot, black-and-white vinyl squares just laid on top of the carpet in checkerboard

fashion. They can just be stacked up and put away later.

Bob also defines an area by installing a border, such as white pillars ("The Snow Queen") or rose topiaries ("Alice in Wonderland").

4) Never pay retail!
The first step of your buying strategy is to *look at what you already have.* Bob works with the staff at Lyndhurst to incorporate furnishings from the museum's collection into the fairy-tale rooms. Other items are loaned or donated by friends.

Above: With the Snow Queen's tree in place, Bob Pesce slides mirror tiles into place over the regular flooring to make her frozen lake. Below: Once the tiles are down, he covers their edges with faux snow. Below left: In the sketch, garlands are planned for the window and mantel. Opposite: Bob directs a garland installation.

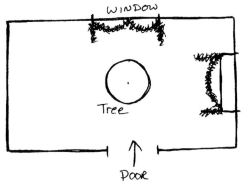

Left: A garland for Snow-White's room has clumps of fake snow on top, several red bead garlands hung in swags, and a red-and-gold bow at each corner.

Hanging from the ends of the garland are red bead chains, draped to look like tassels.

Below: Making a compote of faux fruit.

Below left: Bunching icicle ornaments for realism.

hot glue each ring of fruit to previous row

cardboard circle base cut to fit compote

fill gaps with leaves and smaller fruit

Icicle and drop-shaped ornaments hung on the ends of swag branch

Buy on sale and mix the cheap with the treasure. Some high-quality ornaments in the fairy-tale exhibit were collected over the years at sample sales, greatly discounted. Other ornaments and props, such as faux-stone planters, were cheapies bought for the occasion. Watch for sales both before and after Christmas. There are also Internet suppliers with huge selections and discount prices (see "Sources," page 158).

Turn non-ornaments into ornaments. Ornaments can be made from things intended for another use, such as the sachets that became little mattress ornaments for "The Princess and the Pea." The playing-card garland on Alice's tree is made from the red cards in an ordinary deck, hot-glued into a purchased garland. (See diagrams, page 156.) The "Alice" ornament on page 105 is an image cut from a greeting card, with a cord glued on.

Items left over from an unrelated decorating or craft project can also turn into ornaments or props.

Think big. A 7-foot tree at Lyndhurst may display as many as 200 ornaments. The impact of a tree is strongest if the scale of certain decorations is big. Using very large balls near the bottom or 4-inch-wide ribbon on the garland will make your decorations look much grander. This takes nerve, but it makes the difference between nondescript and spectacular.

Recycle where you can. In the "Alice" room, one year's pink velvet table-topper became the next year's tree skirt after it was slit with scissors from one edge to the middle.

. . . But never skimp on the ribbons. While you can sometimes get away with a low-end Christmas ball in the right color, never use cheap-looking ribbons. Bob uses generous lengths of silk *Dupioni* ribbons in solid jewel colors, usually 3 or 4 inches wide. They are probably the most prominent feature of the display, and give it a magnificent, opulent quality.

The principle is to spend the money where it shows and not where it doesn't. If you see something truly spectacular, get enough so you can use it generously.

5) Budget your time (and work fast).

The 15-room display at Lyndhurst has to be set up in the space of a week by Bob and a few assistants. He has no time to waste. So he uses *pre-lit, artificial trees*, and he doesn't decorate the backs if they don't show. Artificial trees last longer and are less likely to damage museum collections. You can bend and shape the branches to make garlands hang more evenly. And you can also pull branches aside to create an open area, making a little scene or diorama right on the tree. (See Little Red Riding Hood's tree, page 51.)

Almost all Bob's tricks also work on real trees, but you have to allow more time and adapt your designs to the tree. For example, you can't bend branches to make the diorama just mentioned, but you can take advantage of an existing gap or make one with clippers.

Bob uses artificial pine garlands in standard lengths of 8 or 9 feet, rather than spending time cutting them to fit. A very large archway or window will use two, joined in the middle.

Go with other people's enthusiasm. Cathryn Anders, Lyndhurst's assistant director, has plenty of other duties on her plate, but inspiration got the better of

A can light is just visible at lower right, shining on the compote and the garland above it in The Little Mermaid's room.

her, and she made the Seven Dwarfs' hats and boots from her stash of felt at home. (For the pattern, see "Sources," page 158.) When you do something fun, other people often volunteer their ideas and talents.

6) Let there be Lighting!

Everyone has Christmas lights, but the use of light in the Lyndhurst display puts it in another universe.

What is lit, will be seen. If Bob thinks a tree should have more illumination, he sometimes adds a string of colored "novelty" lights around the outside of the tree or on the tree's garland. Or he may install an extra string of regular lights stuffed near the trunk, so the tree glows from within.

Some rooms have "can lights," aimed to shine on the tree. Their job is to make a key feature glow—like a stage spot on a star actor. Purchased from a lighting or hardware store, they are plugged into the nearest outlet and placed on the floor behind a door or piece of furniture. Can lights are especially useful if the room itself is dimly lit, or if a tree has no lights—such as when it is decorated with fake snow and a string of lights might create a fire hazard.

A little colored tinsel stuffed among the branches will reflect even more light. The full, sparkling impact is most magical at night.

7) Have fun!

Playfulness is the hallmark of a fairy-tale scene. For instance, fairy tales play games with size: Beauty's goblet in the "Beauty and the Beast" room is actually a shrimp compote. It's about twice the size of a regular goblet. Other magical things can be teeny-tiny—such as a miniature scene set up in a cabinet near your tree.

When a room is almost done, Bob looks it over to see if it needs an extra touch—for instance, stuffing an extra piece of bubble wrap in the Mermaid's bathtub to increase the watery glow. He also doesn't hesitate to remove elements that aren't working.

You're working from a plan—but *part of the plan is to improvise and follow the magic.*

SET-UP SECRETS
Safety first.

There is no substitute for common sense. Test any new lighting situations. Don't keep a heavily decorated tree lit when you leave the house. If a tree looks unstable, secure it by a guy-wire to an inconspicuous piece of hardware nearby, such as a window latch or an unused doorknob. If you have an active household, you can substitute a piece of mylar or sheets of iridescent wrap instead of mirrors for the Snow Queen's lake. There is no getting around the fact that what may be fine and fun in one house is a recipe for disaster in another. Be aware of situations or people in your house that may require special consideration (such as two-year-olds), and adapt your design accordingly.

Do things in the right order.

Just as if you were painting a room, *install your decorations at the higher, harder-to-reach places first* and work your way toward the door, using your diagram as a guide. Pine garlands are usually easier to place and decorate before the tree goes up—you won't be bumping into the tree with your ladder. *Attach them over doors and windows with floral wire*, which is twisted around nails inconspicuously hammered into the top of the moldings—one nail in the center and one at each side usually does it. (More nails or a staple here and there may be helpful if the span is long.)

To protect a fine mantelpiece, a heavy garland can be attached to a felt-covered board that sits on the mantel. Lighter garlands are draped and held in place with nylon fishing line. Sticky-backed velcro strips can also be used to hold things in place.

Lay down any special flooring that actually goes under the tree. But note that some floor decorations, such as Snow-White's snow bank, are easier to add later, since the tree doesn't sit on them.

Set up the tree, fluffing out the branches so they look as natural as possible. *Note:* Artificial trees have a chemical on them

that can dry out skin after prolonged exposure; use hand cream as needed.

If you're using a real tree, string the lights now. Add additional lights to a pre-lit one if desired.

Drape the tree with some kind of garland. You can use either ribbons, "novelty" garlands, or both (for possible styles, see diagram opposite).

On the trees in "Peter Pan" and "The Princess and the Pea," the ribbons hang down from the top like streamers on a Maypole. They are twisted or pinched in periodically as they wrap around the tree, so they drape gracefully, rather than hanging stiffly. A small bow or loop can be used to cover each pinch along the way.

Glue caps on ornaments.

For high-speed professional decorating, Bob and his assistants *hot-glue the caps on all the ornaments before they are hung for the first time.* If the caps are secure, the ornaments aren't knocked off and destroyed as easily, and there is less hazard from broken glass.

Pile ornaments on the floor.

Put all the apples together, all the red bead chains, and so on. Then divide each pile into four equal groups. This will make it easier to distribute each type of ornament evenly around the tree; the same principle applies to ornaments used on pine garlands.

Square
← 3½" →

Left and below: Making mattress ornaments for "The Princess and the Pea." Bottom of page: A garland for "Alice in Wonderland" begins with a deck of cards and a string.

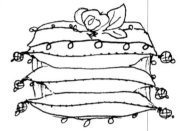

purchased "mirror" garland

garland for Alice's tree — red cards hot glued

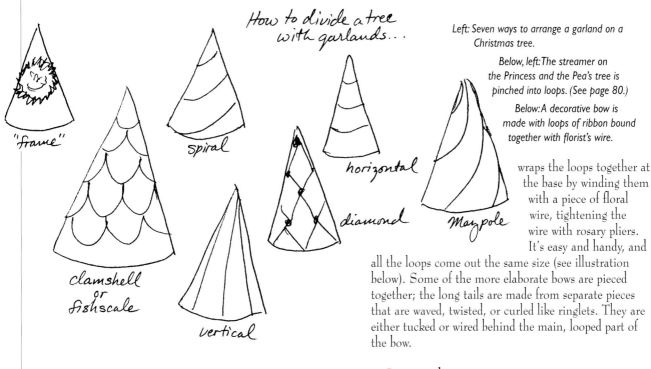

How to divide a tree
with garlands...

"frame"

spiral

clamshell
or
fishscale

vertical

horizontal

diamond

Maypole

Left: Seven ways to arrange a garland on a Christmas tree.

Below, left: The streamer on the Princess and the Pea's tree is pinched into loops. (See page 80.)

Below: A decorative bow is made with loops of ribbon bound together with florist's wire.

wraps the loops together at the base by winding them with a piece of floral wire, tightening the wire with rosary pliers. It's easy and handy, and all the loops come out the same size (see illustration below). Some of the more elaborate bows are pieced together; the long tails are made from separate pieces that are waved, twisted, or curled like ringlets. They are either tucked or wired behind the main, looped part of the bow.

Last touches.

An additional garland can be draped on the tree after the ornaments are in place, plus any final touches—such as artificial snowflakes for extra sparkle.

Then move in any remaining props or furniture around the tree to complete your scene.

A FINAL NOTE

By now you should be saying to yourself, "Oh, I'd do *that* part differently!" This is where the real fun comes in. Everyone's interests vary, so each display is unique.

Consider this book a jump-start for the imagination. Mix elements from different chapters, change colors, or focus on another aspect of a tale.

The pile of ornaments you find on sale may be different from any pictured in this book. Maybe you will simply adapt your family's existing stash of favorites. You'll bring in branches from outside to decorate a forest for Hansel and Gretel—or hang pretty silver spider-web ornaments on Sleeping Beauty's tree, combining the fairy tale with an Eastern European tradition.

Now that I think of it, with less snow and more feathers, maybe the Snow Queen's room could be turned into Swan Lake . . .

Don't use hangers.

As you start hanging the ornaments on the tree, **use floral wire instead of ornament hangers.** Take a piece of wire about 4 inches long, loop the ornament on it and twist it around the branch—like a twist-tie closing a bag of bread. Small ornaments are hung in bundles of two or three on the same wire. It saves time and makes them hang more beautifully, like a bunch of fruit on a branch. This imitation of nature is one of the most important details of a good-looking tree. Icicle- or drop-shaped ornaments are hung from the ends of branches or garlands—as if they dripped down and froze there (see illustration, page 154).

Ornaments with a thread-loop hanger are looped over the branch and then wrapped around several times until all the string is gone. The ornament should look as if it's just touching the branch—not hanging by a string.

Beautiful bows.

Bob makes his big bows by wrapping each loop around his leg, just above the knee to shape it. Then he

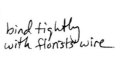

add as many loops as desired

bind tightly with florist's wire

Sources

Lyndhurst
A National Trust Historic Site
635 South Broadway, Tarrytown, N.Y.
(914) 631-4481. Take the virtual tour
and find out about this grand Hudson
River mansion just 20 miles north of
New York City. *www.lyndhurst.org*

A Fairy-Tale Christmas
The official *A Fairy-Tale Christmas*
Web site, where you can find more
fairy-tale recipes, crafts, and celebrations. You can send me e-mail there, too.
www.afairytalechristmas.com

Bryan E. McCay Photography
Bryan took the photographs in this
book. For more of his pictures, see:
www.bryanmccayphotography.com

R.A. (Bob) Pesce
Bob, who designed and installed the
exhibits at Lyndhurst, is best reached by
e-mail:. *RAPesce@aol.com*

STYLE and FOOD
Afloral.com (888) 299-4100
Floral wire (24 gauge), silk flowers,
poinsettias, seashells, seashell garlands,
and other floral supplies at discount
prices (general). *www.afloral.com*

Hearthsong (800) 325-2502
Alligator-themed toys such as the 3-
D puzzle on page 116, as well as pirate
games and rope ladders (Peter Pan).
www.hearthsong.com

Jewelry Supply.com
(916) 780-9610
Rosary pliers—used for twisting
wire around things and pulling the wire
tight around bow loops (general).
www.jewelrysupply.com

JKM Ribbon & Trims
Silk *Dupioni* wired ribbon sold by
the spool at good discounts. Minimum
order $25; no phone orders (general).
www.jkmribbon.com

Magic Cabin (888) 623-6557
Wool felt in a wide variety of colors
for making dwarf hats and boots; red
cotton velour cloak (Snow White; Little
Red Riding Hood). *www.magiccabin.com*

Merchant Overstock
(800) 433-0038
Pre-lit artificial trees and garlands;
Kurt Adler diamond iridescent & silver
bead garland (Sleeping Beauty; The
Princess and the Pea). *www.merchan-
toverstock.com*

Michaels (800) 642-4235
Christmas ornaments and supplies,
seasonally. Sea shells, floral supplies,
wire, tools, and Wilton baking supplies
(The Little Mermaid, Alice in Wonderland; general styling). *www.michaels.com*

**National Trust for Historic
Preservation** (800) 944-6847
Besides Lyndhurst, the National
Trust owns and operates 25 other
historic locations throughout the nation.
www.nationaltrust.org

Northern Brewer
(800) 681-2739
Dried sweet woodruff (Little Red
Riding Hood). *www.northernbrewer.com*

**Oren's Daily Roast Coffees &
Teas** (212) 348-5400
Ethiopian Longberry Harrar and
Yergacheffe coffees (The Nutcracker
Ballet). *www.orensdailyroast.com*

Pier 1 Imports (800) 245-4595
Craquelle glassware (The Snow
Queen). *www.pier1.com*

Simpson & Vail (800) 282-8327
Specialty tea and coffee importers.
Ethiopian coffees, Russian "firebird" teapot and cups (The Nutcracker Ballet).
www.svtea.com

L. E. Smith Glass Company
(800) 537-6484
Trellis pattern glassware (Alice in
Wonderland). *www.lesmithglass.com*

Sweet Celebrations
(800) 328-6722
Coin molds, chocolate, gold and
colored foil wrappers (Rumpelstiltskin;
Sleeping Beauty). *www.sweetc.com*

Williams-Sonoma
(877) 812-6235
Unusual china (Beauty and the Beast;
Sleeping Beauty; The Princess and the
Pea). *www.williams-sonoma.com*

FAIRY-TALE INTERPRETERS
Thanks to Dr. Philip Mango of **St.
Michael's Institute for the Psy-
chological Sciences** for his insights
on psychology in Dickens's *A Christmas
Carol. www.saintmichael.net*

Thanks to Arthur Fredrick and the
Danbury Music Centre of Danbury,
Connecticut, a community-based group
that performs *The Nutcracker* at Christmastime every year in its true spirit.
www.danbury.org/musicctr

**FAIRY-TALE BOOKS,
ARTICLES, and WEB SITES**
Ashliman, D.L. **Folklore and
Mythology Electronic Texts.**
For comparative texts and translations
of many of the tales in this book, plus
related folk-tales. *www.pitt.edu/~dash/
folktexts.html*

Gray, Doug. **Christian Symbols
and Their Meanings.** (Snow-
White) *www.christiansymbols.net*

Heiner, Heidi Anne. "A Fairy-Tale
Timeline," **Sur la Lune Fairy-Tale
Pages.** (Cinderella) *www.surlalunefairy-
tales.com*

Lowin, Dr. Joseph. "A Hebrew
Lesson: Crown," **Jewish Heritage
Online Magazine.** (The Nutcracker
Ballet) *www.jhom.com*

Moss, Simon. "Peter Pan: A Selling
Exhibition of Memorabilia," **C20th.**
For information on the original
stage production and script of *Peter Pan. www.
c20th.com*

Murphy, G. Ronald. **The Owl,
the Raven, and the Dove.** New
York: Oxford University Press, 2002.
(Snow-White, Hansel and Gretel, and
other tales, plus general biographical
information on the Grimms)

Owens-Celli, Morgyn Geoffry. **The
Book of Wheat Weaving and
Straw Craft.** New York: Sterling,
1998. (Rumpelstiltskin and the cultural
history and mythology of wheat)

Tyghe, William J. "Calculating Christmas," **Touchstone.** (A Christmas
Carol) *http://touchstonemag.com*

Wiener, Hesh. "The Princess and IP,"
IT Jungle. (The Princess and the Pea)
www.itjungle.com

Zimmer, Melanie. **Dancing Bear
Puppet Theater.** For background on
tales and authors. *www.thepuppets.com*

BOOKS on JAY GOULD
Klein, Maury. **The Life and Leg-
end of Jay Gould.** Baltimore, Md.:
Johns Hopkins University Press, 1986.
(Notes from an Enchanted Castle)

Renehan, Jr., Edward J. **Dark
Genius of Wall Street: *The
Misunderstood Life of Jay Gould,
King of the Robber Barons.*** New
York: Basic Books, 2005. (Notes from an
Enchanted Castle)

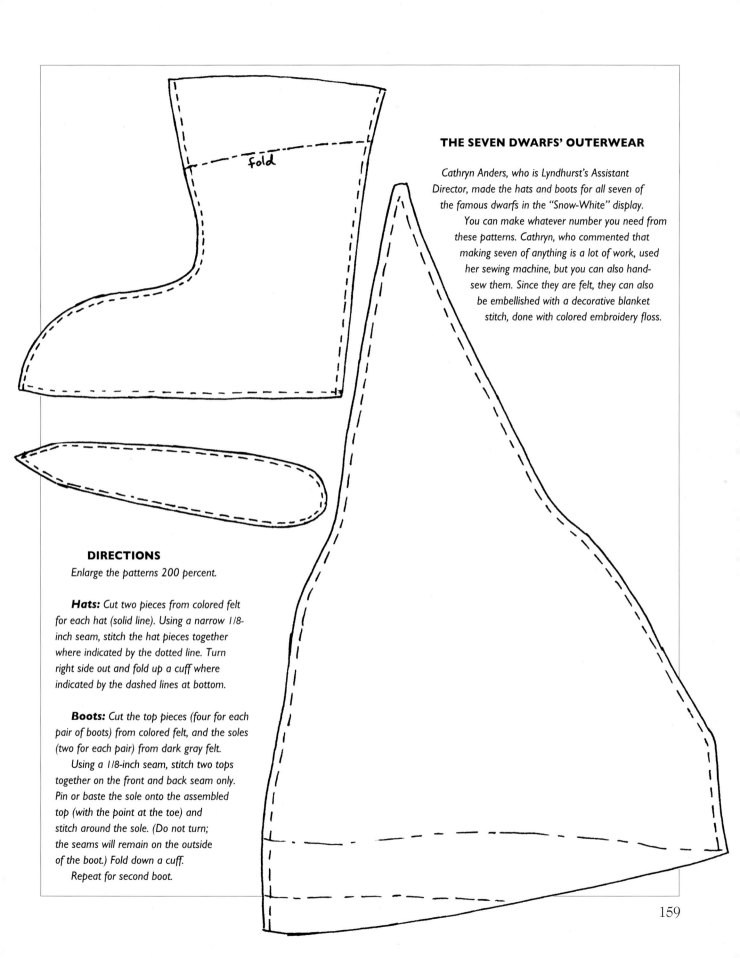

fold

THE SEVEN DWARFS' OUTERWEAR

Cathryn Anders, who is Lyndhurst's Assistant Director, made the hats and boots for all seven of the famous dwarfs in the "Snow-White" display. You can make whatever number you need from these patterns. Cathryn, who commented that making seven of anything is a lot of work, used her sewing machine, but you can also hand-sew them. Since they are felt, they can also be embellished with a decorative blanket stitch, done with colored embroidery floss.

DIRECTIONS

Enlarge the patterns 200 percent.

Hats: *Cut two pieces from colored felt for each hat (solid line). Using a narrow 1/8-inch seam, stitch the hat pieces together where indicated by the dotted line. Turn right side out and fold up a cuff where indicated by the dashed lines at bottom.*

Boots: *Cut the top pieces (four for each pair of boots) from colored felt, and the soles (two for each pair) from dark gray felt.*

Using a 1/8-inch seam, stitch two tops together on the front and back seam only. Pin or baste the sole onto the assembled top (with the point at the toe) and stitch around the sole. (Do not turn; the seams will remain on the outside of the boot.) Fold down a cuff.

Repeat for second boot.